Dr Tony Fincham, a vice-president and former chairman of the Thomas Hardy Society, has been exploring Hardy's Wessex for forty years, during which time he has led many walks through Hardy Country and has lectured widely on Hardy's landscape. His previous publications include *Hardy's Landscape Revisited* (Hardy's Wessex in the Twenty-First Century) and *Hardy the Physician*, a medical interpretation of Hardy's life and works. Tony works as a GP in rural West Kent, where he lives with his partner Mary and Dalmatians, Eddie and Lizzie.

Following pages
Looking south over the Marshwood Vale from Pilsdon Pen:
'There are some heights in Wessex, shaped as if by a kindly hand/
For thinking, dreaming, dying on.'

THE DOVECOTE PRESS

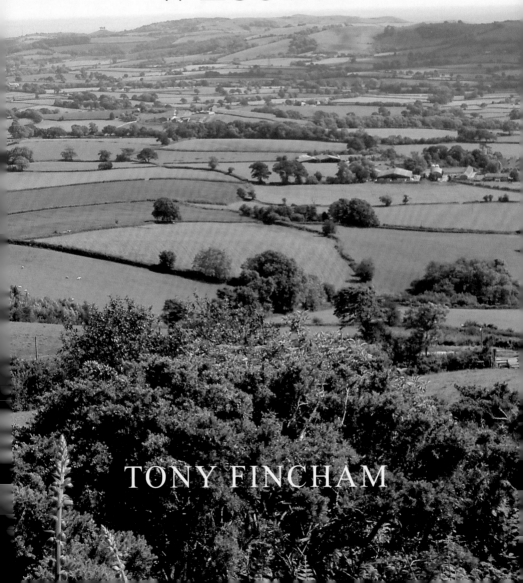

Exploring
Thomas Hardy's
WESSEX

TONY FINCHAM

First published in 2016 by The Dovecote Press Ltd
Stanbridge, Wimborne Minster, Dorset BH21 4JD

ISBN 978-0-9929151-5-5

Typeset in FS Ingrid and designed by The Dovecote Press Ltd
Printed and bound in Spain by GraphyCems, Navarra
All papers used by The Dovecote Press are natural, recyclable products
made from wood grown in sustainable, well-managed forests.

A CLP catalogue record for this book is available from the British Library

1 3 5 7 9 8 6 4 2

Contents

ONE

Introduction

Thomas Hardy was born in Bockhampton in rural Dorset in June 1840; he died at the house he built for himself, Max Gate, just outside Dorchester in January 1928. In the intervening 88 years, he wrote and published 14 novels, over 50 short stories, an epic verse-drama and nearly 1,000 poems. The frail boy from an obscure Dorset hamlet became in time the much-feted grand old man of English letters, given a funeral in Westminster Abbey, where his ten pall-bearers included the prime minister and the literary greats of the day. This fame was achieved mainly on the strength of his novels, published between 1870 and 1897; tales of life, love and betrayal set in the rural community of his childhood, often based upon true incidents from what he described as 'the immediately recoverable past'. By the end of his life, the Victorian novelist, a contemporary of Dickens, had become a 20th century poet, a contemporary of T. S. Eliot.

Hardy's stories were set in 'the part real, part dream country' for which he chose the name Wessex, after King Alfred's Saxon kingdom. So successful has Hardy's resurrection of this once obsolete term become that Wessex is now restored to common usage. In defining Wessex, Hardy not only marked out his fictional territory but gave each individual place its own separate name, often based upon historic designations, to emphasise the distinction between fiction and reality. Thus there have been several hundred Mayors of Dorchester but only three fictional Mayors of Casterbridge.

The first collected edition of Hardy's works (1895) was accompanied by a detailed map of Wessex, which is illustrated on page 9. This whole process can be seen as a shrewd and most successful marketing device. Literary tourism came on apace with the growth of Romanticism; for the reader to be moved to tears by the fate of Tess d'Urberville or Bathsheba Everdene and then to be able to visit the places where these heroines lived, loved and died gives an entire extra dimension to the literary experience, especially when these scenes are set amongst some of the most beautiful countryside in England. 120 years after Hardy published his last novel, literary pilgrims still journey to Dorset and the adjoining counties to discover for themselves the landscape of his fiction and poetry. This book is designed to facilitate and enhance such exploration of Hardy's Wessex.

To gain the most from this book, use it in conjunction with OS Explorer maps Sheets OL 15 'Purbeck & South Dorset' and 117 'Cerne Abbas & Bere Regis', which cover the vast majority of Hardy's landscapes. Also, a copy of *The Complete Poems of Thomas Hardy,*

Above Thomas Hardy OM in 1923 aged 83 – now the grand old man of English Literature. From the painting by Augustus John.

Above Thomas Hardy in 1856 aged 16, son of a local stone mason and newly appointed apprentice to the architect John Hicks in Dorchester.

edited by James Gibson, will add to your enjoyment and understanding of the writer and his works. References to relevant poems are given throughout this book as (CPxxx); the xxx representing the poem number in the Gibson volume. Hardy's Wessex places names are printed in bold; and I have included a detailed list of them at the end of this book. A second glossary links characters to Hardy's works.

For the ideal visual introduction to Hardy's Wessex, take the train from Southampton to Weymouth, passing Southampton Water, The New Forest, Poole Harbour, The Purbeck Hills, Bindon Abbey Mill (Tess), Egdon Heath, Max Gate, Dorchester (**Casterbridge**) to reach Weymouth (**Budmouth**).

When is the best time of year to explore Wessex? In winter and early spring the going may be muddy, but the views are at their best, allowing buildings to be seen more clearly, and whole landscape vistas to open before your eyes. Hardy, above all, is a 'landscape novelist'. Spring and early summer are glorious for the wild flowers, which add to the attractiveness of many of the walks and routes described in the book, especially as many include backwater country lanes whose verges and hedges are largely left uncut. Autumn is also good, for many of the best-known scenes in the novels take place then, and the countryside is more peaceful without the summer visitors.

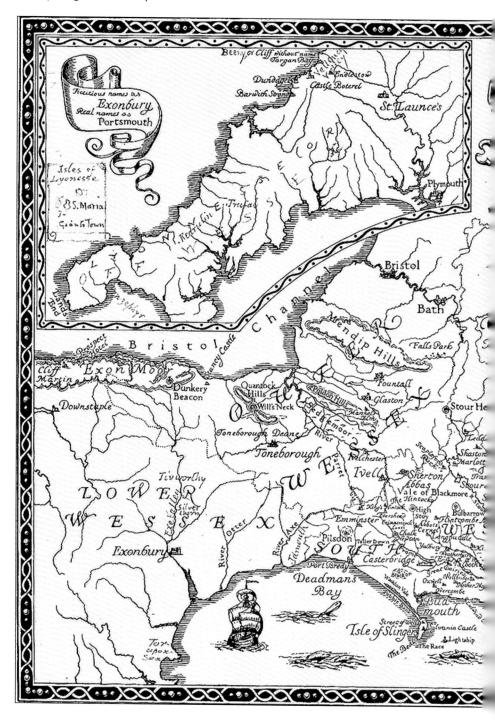

In 1895 Hardy drew a map of Wessex to show all the places mentioned in his novels, using their fictional names. Alongside he wrote, 'It is to be understood that this is an imaginative Wessex only, & that the places described under the names here given are not portraits of any real places, but visionary places which may approximate to the real places more or less.'

This version of the map was drawn by William Morris's printer, Emery Walker, to accompany an edition of the collected novels.

TWO

Higher Bockhampton and Egdon Heath

By car, using OS Explorer 15, start your exploration from Thorncombe Wood Car Park; off Cuckoo Lane (NGR SY726921). By foot, retrace the young Thomas Hardy's route along public footpaths from Dorchester via Stinsford and Kingston Maurward. The new Visitor Centre, situated on the corner of the lane which leads to the Hardys' Cottage is a great starting point for information about Hardy, his life and works. For the more atmospheric route from the Car Park to the Cottage, follow the signposted track through wood.

The Hardys' Cottage, built in 1800 by Thomas' great-grandfather John Hardy, was the first dwelling in Higher Bockhampton; its appearance closely fits Hardy's description of the Tranter's house in *Under the Greenwood Tree* (see opposite page). The cottage was built as two separate dwellings; the original extending from the central chimney stack to the lane with just two rooms above and one below. The extension southwards was built to accommodate Hardy's grandmother Mary on his parents' marriage (1839). Later, the two halves were joined together and the present off-centre front door added. The second

The new Visitor Centre for Hardy's Birthplace provides useful information about Hardy and Egdon; toilets and refreshments.

The Hardys' Cottage: 'It was a long low cottage with a hipped roof of thatch, having dormer windows breaking up into the eaves, a chimney standing in the middle of the ridge and another at each end'.

Hardy's mother, Jemima, with her eldest son, Thomas, as a baby.

window from the left marks the site of the original entrance door, described in the poem 'The Self-Unseeing' (CP135). This door opened straight from the garden into the large parlour; scene of lively Christmas dances in *Under the Greenwood Tree* and *The Return of the Native;* where Eustacia and the mummers are trapped in the frosty garden because 'the door opens right upon the front sitting-room' in 'this quaint old habitation' and to open the door would stop the dance. The outhouses to the right were the scene of cider-making, described in both *Desperate Remedies* and *Under the Greenwood Tree*.

Hardy was born at 8am on 2 June 1840 in the central of the three upstairs chambers, after a long and difficult labour. The baby, initially cast aside as dead, was to develop from a precocious toddler into a bright, questioning, observant young child. In his early years, Hardy slept in the left-hand bedroom, shared with his sister Mary. He later moved into his

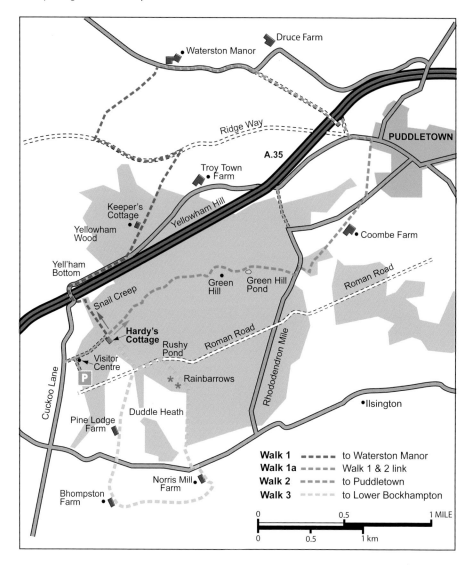

Druce Farm

Waterston Manor

Ridge Way

PUDDLETOWN

A.35

Troy Town Farm

Keeper's Cottage

Yellowham Wood

Yellowham Hill

Coombe Farm

Yell'ham Bottom

Snail Creep

Green Hill

Green Hill Pond

Roman Road

Hardy's Cottage

Rushy Pond

Roman Road

Rhododendron Mile

Visitor Centre

Rainbarrows

Ilsington

Cuckoo Lane

Pine Lodge Farm

Duddle Heath

Norris Mill Farm

Bhompston Farm

Walk 1 - - - - - to Waterston Manor
Walk 1a - - - - - Walk 1 & 2 link
Walk 2 - - - - - to Puddletown
Walk 3 - - - - - to Lower Bockhampton

| 0 | 0.5 | 1 MILE |
| 0 | 0.5 | 1 km |

grandmother's former bedroom (right-hand window); here at the window-seat he wrote his early fiction, including *Far from the Madding Crowd*. The success of this novel, published in 1874, allowed him to marry and move away, but his heart remained at Bockhampton and on the Heath: he regularly returned to the cottage for the rest of his long life. Many poems relate to the cottage, especially *'Domicilium'* (CP1), Hardy's Wordsworthian earliest surviving poem; and *'When I Set Out for Lyonnesse'* (CP254), Hardy's recollection of his first magical trip to Cornwall (see also CPs 222, 320, 433, 551, 791, 839). Wander around the cottage garden, ever-evolving under the careful husbandry of the National Trust,

Behind the Cottage: The fingerpost offering A35/ Puddletown/ Lower Bockhampton. Beside it, there is a 'monument erected to his memory by a few of his American Admirers 1931'.

absorb the atmosphere, then leave the garden to note the American Memorial; beside it is a wooden fingerpost whose choices offer three different Hardy walks.

Walk 1: To the left: path labelled 'A 35': head up through beech trees along a beautiful undulating woodland track. This is Snail Creep, where Dick Dewy went nutting without Fancy; descend towards the bypass, cross it by the Cuckoo Lane bridge, obtaining very clear views of the destruction wrought upon Puddletown Heath/Forest by the road builders: and as the flyover curves round, turn left onto the old main road. This is Yell'ham Bottom (CP261), where Henchard tried unsuccessfully to persuade Farfrae to return to his dying wife in the aftermath of the skimmety ride. Ahead lies Yellowham Hill and Yalbury Wood; home to the Wild Man o'Yall'm, held responsible for fathering many of the 'love-children' born in the neighbouring villages. Beyond Vaughan Agri, take the bridleway on the left into the wood to soon reach Keeper's Cottage (*see next page*), which stands precisely as Hardy describes it, grass in front and great trees behind, one of which was the 'Greenwood Tree' under which Dick and Fancy's wedding was celebrated with feasting and country dances. This cottage, with thickly leaded diamond glazing as described by Hardy, was home to Keeper Browne, whose daughter inspired '*To Lizbie Browne*' (CP130). From Keeper's Cottage, if you continue on the same track uphill, you reach the Ridgeway, from where a left and then right turn will lead you down to Waterston Manor, home of Bathsheba Everdene in *Far from the Madding Crowd*.

Keeper's Cottage: 'Geoffrey Day lived in the depths of Yalbury Wood, which formed portion of one of the outlying estates of the Earl of Wessex, to whom Day was head gamekeeper.'

Walk 2: The sandy track straight ahead marked 'Puddletown', takes you into the heart of that 'vast tract of unenclosed wild', **Egdon Heath**. In *The Return of the Native*, Hardy, at the time himself a returned native, describes Clym Yeobright as having 'been so interwoven with the Heath in his boyhood that hardly anybody could look upon it without thinking of him.'

For 'if anyone knew the heath well it was Clym. He was permeated with its scenes, with its substance, and with its odours. He might be said to be its product. His eyes had first opened thereon; with its appearance all the images of his memory were mingled. His toys had been the flint knives and arrow-heads which he found there. His flowers the purple bells and yellow gorse; his animal kingdom the snakes and croppers; his society its human haunters'. For Clym, read Hardy.

Egdon Heath was defined by Hardy's favoured topographer Hermann Lea as 'That vast expanse of moorland which stretches, practically without a break, from Dorchester to Bournemouth.' Desmond Hawkins interpreted 'this severe unwelcoming landscape with its strange beauty and untameable character' as 'one of the grand metaphors of Hardy's imagination: a symbol of Nature's indifference to human frustration and despair'. Hardy opens *The Return of the Native* with a detailed description of the Heath, which can be regarded as the main character in the novel: 'The untameable, Ishmaelitish thing that Egdon now was it always had been. Civilization was its enemy. Ever since the beginning

Although naive, Hardy's own painting 'Rainbarrow and the Heath' (1871), captures his description of it as this 'obscure, obsolete, superseded country features in Domesday: heathy, furzy, briary wilderness.'

Unspoilt Egdon: 'A place perfectly accordant with man's nature: neither ghastly, hateful nor ugly: neither commonplace, unmeaning nor tame, but like man slighted and enduring.' (*Return of the Native*).

of vegetation its soil had worn the same antique brown dress. The great inviolate place had an ancient permanence which the sea cannot claim. Who can say of a particular sea that it is old? Distilled by the sun, kneaded by the moon, it is renewed in a year, in a day, or in an hour. The sea changed, the fields changed, the rivers, the villages and the people changed yet Egdon remained.'

The Heath behind **Blooms-End**: 'Snakes and efts,/ Swarmed in the summer days and nightly bats/ Would fly about our bedrooms. Heathcroppers/ lived on the hills, and were our only friends.' (CP1)

Where is this Egdon waste now? Civilization was its enemy for it has fallen prey to four main human activities: the army, afforestation, enclosure for agriculture and house building (these activities in order of increasing destructiveness). Contrary to the impression which Hardy gives, heathland is managed land. Although lowland heathland is internationally recognised as an endangered habitat, it is estimated that 1.5 acres of **Egdon** is being lost daily, mainly to development. Approximately 10,000 unspoilt acres remain today, of which nearly a quarter is on MoD property and thus relatively secure, although inaccessible. Afforestation had begun in Hardy's time but accelerated with the establishment of the Forestry Commission in 1919, whose stated aim was to turn 'non-productive' heathland into 'productive' conifer plantations'. So the vast open vistas of unspoilt Egdon described in *The Return of the Native* have been replaced by dark stands of conifer. Recently, there have been limited attempts to restore the heath immediately behind Hardy's Cottage and around **Rainbarrow**.

Follow the track straight on behind Hardy's Cottage to reach Green Hill, probable site of **Mistover Knap**, home to Eustacia Vye and 'the loneliest of lonely houses on these thinly populated slopes'. On your right, beyond the crest of the hill lies Green Hill Pond, most likely candidate for the pond beside Eustacia's house. Continue down to Rhododendron Mile, then bear left and soon right on to the bridleway which passes through a wood to reach Coombe Farm, favourite place for local dancing, described by Hardy as 'gipsyings',

Rushy Pond. in winter. Hardy carried the family 'big brass telescope' here to watch an execution nearly three miles away; the roofs of Dorchester Prison being then clearly visible.

and recorded '*In a Eweleaze near Weatherbury*' (CP47). From here the bridleway leads onto Puddletown (**Weatherbury**), home to many of Hardy's cousins. Tracks branching off from this route allow a full exploration of **Egdon**, except to the north where all the old footpaths come to an abrupt halt at the A35 dual-carriageway, whose raucous sounds drown out the sweet melodies of the heath.

Walk 3: To the right, signposted 'Lower Bockhampton': pass directly behind the cottage, noting the small window used for paying workmen their weekly wages, and bearing left at the signpost, follow the wooded track to Rushy Pond. This idyllic spot, only a few hundred yards from the cottage, was known intimately to Hardy as a child. Here read '*At Rushy Pond*' (CP680) and the similar earlier '*Neutral Tones*' (CP 9), set at Tolmare Pond near Findon.

Cross the barrier behind the pond to follow the footpath along '*The Roman Road*' (CP218), an overgrown but well-preserved section of the road which ran from Dorchester to Salisbury. As the road ends, take the track to the right across Duddle Heath, which has been extensively cleared, allowing the Bronze Age Rainbarrows to re-emerge from the deep coniferous cover, which had obscured them for 80 years.

Beyond the first two tumuli, a gated path leads to Hardy's **Rainbarrow** which stands on the crest of the ridge, surmounted by a holly tree. Here Diggory Venn in *The Return of the Native* notices a motionless Eustacia scanning the horizon. Ahead of her, in the distance, the chalk downs obscured Osmington Bay, where 'hill hid tides throb throe on throe' (CP563). To the left, on a clear day, there are extensive views to the Purbeck

'The Roman Road runs straight and bare/ As the pale parting-line in hair/ Across the heath. And thoughtful men/ Contrast its days of Now and Then,/ And delve, and measure, and compare;/ Visioning on the vacant air/ Helmed legionaries.'

Hills and right to the Hardy Monument on Blackdown. Closer to and sharp right Kingston Maurward House dominates the middle distance; beyond it are the chimneys and spires of **Casterbridge**, at times magically illuminated by the early morning sun. Tess, approaching **Talbothays**, compares the landscape below with her native Blackmoor and notes that 'the world was drawn on a larger pattern here'. The extensive woods further east obscure **Shadwater Weir**, site of the tragic culmination of *The Return of the Native*. The track beside **Rainbarrow** leads down from **Egdon** into Hardy's **Valley of the Great Dairies**.

East Egdon: it is easy to follow Mrs Yeobright's fatal last walk by taking the signposted track from behind her home (**Blooms-End**/Hardy's Cottage) to Puddletown, then the bridleway from Milom Lane across the largely afforested heath to Affpuddle (**Alderworth**). By car, park in Cullpeppers Dish Car Park (NGR SY815924), take the downhill path from the far left corner to reach Clym's Cottage; above you lie the **Devil's Bellows**, the black knoll where Mrs Yeobright rested, intensely agitated. Rimsmoor Pond is clearly marked on the OS map and easy to find; Okers Pool presents more of a challenge as it is hidden in dense furze about 300 yards north-west of Rimsmoor, but the search is worth the effort!

THREE

Stinsford (Mellstock)

'Mellstock was a parish of considerable acreage, the hamlets composing it lying at a much greater distance from each other than is ordinarily the case. There was Lower Mellstock, the main village; half a mile from this were the church and vicarage, and a few other houses. A mile north-east lay the hamlet of Upper Mellstock, where the tranter lived; and at other points knots of cottages, besides solitary farmsteads and dairies.'

Hardy's fictional **Mellstock** equates very closely with the actual parish of Stinsford; and still does so 180 years after the setting of *Under the Greenwood Tree*. The parish remains large, scattered and thinly-populated, reaching from the heights of Waterston Ridge in the north to the lowly Frome watermeadows in the south. In the west the parish abuts the Fordington end of Dorchester and in the east merges beyond Hardy's Cottage into Puddletown Heath. Grey's Bridge and Ten Hatches Weir span the boundary between county town and rural parish. The population of Stinsford parish today is only 300, which is 70 fewer than in 1840. Stinsford Church lies at the heart of this landscape: by car it is a short distance from the A35 roundabout just east of Dorchester. On foot follow the path through the kissing gate just beyond Grey's Bridge (CP895).

On your left as you enter the churchyard, nestling in the shade of an ancient yew,

Stinsford church framed by stone urns on the gate pillars. Drawn by Hardy as the opening illustration for *Wessex Poems*.

HERE·LIES·THE·HEART·OF
THOMAS·HARDY·O·M
SON·OF·THOMAS·AND·JEMIMA·HARDY

HE·WAS·BORN·AT·UPPER·BOCKHAMPTON·2·JUNE·1840
AND·DIED·AT·MAX·GATE·DORCHESTER·11·JANUARY·1928
HIS·ASHES·REST·IN·POETS·CORNER·WESTMINSTER·ABBEY

Left Hardy wished to be buried at Stinsford. In a bizarre compromise, his heart alone was buried here. His body was cremated and the ashes interred in Poets' Corner, Westminster Abbey.

Below Transformations: 'Portion of this yew/ Is a man my grandsire knew,/ Bosomed here at its foot:/ This branch may be his wife,/ A ruddy human life/ Now turned to a green shoot.'

Hardy's heart lies buried between the remains of his wives, Emma and Florence, flanked on the right by the grave of his parents and to the left by the shared grave of his siblings, Mary, Henry and Kate. The line extends with the graves of his paternal grandparents, his uncle James and then aunt Jane and her daughter, Teresa, long-time church organist; then the slate memorials to the poet C. Day-Lewis and his actress wife Jill Balcon: all undergoing *'Transformations'* (CP410). Behind the yew, is the Old Vicarage where in the study young Tom took confirmation classes and the **Mellstock** Quire confronted the vicar about his scheme for replacing them with a barrel organ.

The poem 'Friends Beyond' (CP36), refers to several characters from *Under the Greenwood Tree*, whose memorials can still be identified; and 'The Choirmaster's Burial' (CP489) is the

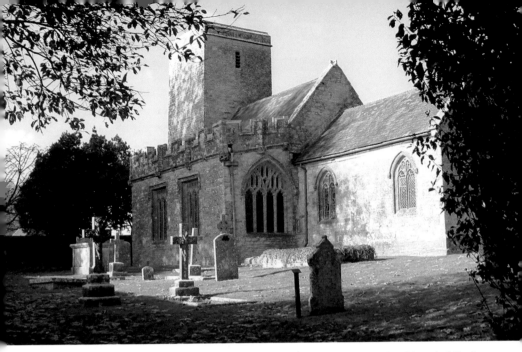

Stinsford Church: in the foreground is the grave of Fanny Hurden, one-time school friend of Hardy. Fanny died aged 20, becoming the inspiration for the tragic Fanny Robin in *Far From the Madding Crowd*. See 'Voices from Things Growing in a Churchyard' (CP580).

story of the internment of Thomas Hardy I, Hardy's grandfather. Throughout his life, Hardy was a regular visitor to his 'Friend's Beyond': as reflected in 'Paying Calls' (CP454), especially after Emma's death as explained in 'Rain on a Grave' (CP280) for 'I have brought her here,/ And have laid her to rest/ In a noiseless nest /No sea beats near' (CP281). See also 'If You Had Known' (CP593) and 'Why She Moved House' (CP806).

As you turn to enter the door in the church tower, the main façade of Stinsford House extends over the wall behind you. This house was long the property of the Strangways family, Earls of Ilchester, whose principle seat is at Melbury House near Evershot. In 1764 the then earl's daughter, Lady Susan, scandalised Society by eloping with William O'Brien, an actor and protégé of David Garrick. Eventually, partially reconciled to the family, they settled at Stinsford House. Hardy's grandfather built a special vault under Stinsford Church for the two lovers; Hardy's father sang for Lady Susan in her old age. The house was subsequently occupied by Revd Edward Murray, an Ilchester relative. Hardy's mother Jemima came to Stinsford House in 1836 as Murray's cook. Here she encountered Thomas Hardy II doing building work on the house. Family tradition has it that Hardy's father promptly seduced her in the bushes by the neighbouring Frome (CP895). The couple did not marry until three years later, Jemima safely pregnant with Thomas III.

Stinsford Church is mainly 13th century. Internally, it has undergone many changes since Hardy's birth, most particularly at the hands of the High Church reformer Arthur

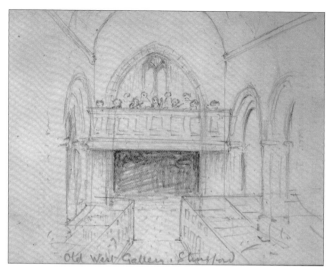

Thomas Hardy's sketch of the Old West Gallery in Stinsford Church. Note the figures of the choir and musicians, and the old box pews in the nave.

Shirley, who succeeded Edward Murray in 1837. The contrasts between Shirley's innovative zeal and Murray's *laissez-faire* are reflected in the contrasts between Parson Maybold and old Mr Grinham in *Under the Greenwood Tree*. Shirley on his arrival increased the number of services, instituted a Sunday school and founded the new National School; all of which had a great influence on Hardy, leading to his deep familiarity with both the Bible and Book of Common Prayer.

Hardy's romantic vision of his parents' first encounter is described in the sonnet 'A Church Romance' (CP211). The west gallery soon fell victim to Shirley's reforming zeal. After 115 years without a west gallery, a splendid new structure was erected in 1996, complete with modern organ which sadly occupies the space needed for the choir. On the wall below the stairs is Hardy's plan of the West Gallery: circa 1835 'Shewing Positions of Choir', including four musicians, Thomas Hardy I and his two sons, plus James Dart on violin. Nearby is the brass tablet put up by Hardy with a Latin inscription commemorating *'Thomae Hardy patris Jacobi et Thomae filiorum'* (1903).

On the north wall, admire the Grey monument with its morbidly realistic skull, which fascinated the young Hardy. On the south wall note the memorial tablet, with its 'two joined hearts enchased there' (CP239) to William O'Brien and Lady Susan, whose earthly remains are buried in their special tomb below; the model for the Luxellian family vault in *A Pair of Blue Eyes*. The Hardy memorial window dominates the south aisle; pause here to read that sadly prophetic poem 'Channel Firing' (CP247), published just three months before the onset of the Great War. As a young man in London in the 1860s, Hardy began to doubt his religious faith: see 'The Impercipient' (CP44) and 'Afternoon Service at Mellstock' (CP356) but he remained, in his own words, 'churchy; not in an intellectual sense, but so far as instincts and emotions ruled'. In his later years, Hardy turned back to

The Hardy memorial window, showing Elijah on Mount Horeb, illustrating 'the earthquake, wind and fire' from I Kings 19, Hardy's favourite biblical passage. (CP371).

The Frome meandering through watermeadows, crossed by the path from Lower to Higher Bockhampton: if the cattle are not grazing these meadows, deer may often be seen.

Stinsford Church as a source of tranquillity, continuity and tradition in a rapidly changing world; as a central focus, second only to the cottage on **Egdon**, of his fiction, his poetry and his imagination; also increasingly as the place where so many of his family, friends, neighbours, and once young women he might have wished to marry, were laid to rest.

A Mellstock Walk (2 miles, OS Explorer 15)

Follow the path from Hardy's grave down towards the lower graveyard, passing on your right the restored headstone of Fanny Hurden, the first of Hardy's 'Voices from Things Growing in a Churchyard' (CP580): memorials to Bachelor Bowring, Thomas Voss, Eve Greensleeves and Squire Grey can also be identified around the church and graveyard. Note also the gargoyles on this side of the church; the most grotesque being in the exact position of the gargoyle on Puddletown church tower which wrecked Fanny's Robin's grave. A corner gate opens from the grassy lower churchyard onto a path down to the Frome. At the junction of paths, turn left along the path between streams. The route straight ahead, signposted 'St George's Road' leads across the watermeadows to Max Gate and was used by Hardy when walking from his home to Stinsford Church; the path to the right was frequented by the young Hardy on his daily walk to-and-from Dorchester (CP895).

Delightful and teeming with nature at all seasons, the Frome-side path leads to Bockhampton Bridge; look downstream to imbibe the atmosphere of Tess's **Valley of the Great Dairies**. Turn left off the bridge into Lower Bockhampton; the first thatched house (Bridge Cottage) originally doubled as blacksmith's and village beer shop; also the lodging of Mop Ollamoor, 'musician, dandy and company-man'. The footpath beside this cottage leads across the watermeadows to Higher Bockhampton. The third thatched cottage on your right was the village post office (CP237). Turn left opposite into Knapwater past the

Kingston Maurward: 'The house was regularly and substantially built of clean grey freestone; a graceful slope running from the terrace to the margin of a placid lake, upon the surface of which a green punt floated at leisure.' (*Desperate Remedies*).

Old School, attended by Hardy from 1848 (CP462); the second halt for the **Mellstock** Quire 'Going the Rounds', where Dick Dewy fell for Fancy Day, 'framed as a picture by the window architrave'. Follow the road into the Kingston Maurward estate, the setting of Hardy's first novel *Desperate Remedies*, encountering first the beautiful old Manor House, in Hardy's day in a very poor state of repair and subdivided into cottages, one of which was occupied by Thomas Way, a dairyman, whose youngest daughter Augusta was spotted by Hardy as she milked the cows in the adjoining byre. Tom was fascinated by the beautiful teenager, who became the model for *Tess of the d'Urbervilles*, and whose daughter Gertrude Bugler was later to play Tess on stage both in Dorchester and London's West End.

Follow the drive down past the weir and bear left towards the front of **Knapwater House**, which appears just as described by Cytherea Graye in *Desperate Remedies*. The new house at Kingston Maurward, built of brick in 1720 by George Pitt, who had married Lora Grey, the last survivor of the family from the old Manor House, was resurfaced in Portland stone in 1794 after George III had derisively exclaimed 'Brick, brick, brick!' In 1845 the Pitt family sold the house to Francis Martin, whose childless wife Julia was particularly attentive to the precocious young Thomas Hardy, who, in return, nourished a romantic attachment to her throughout his adolescence. The gardens of this magnificent house, now an agricultural college, are open to the public daily throughout the year. Follow the drive beyond the house and turn left to retrace your steps to St Michaels' Church.

FOUR

Dorchester & *The Mayor of Casterbridge*

From the age of ten until just before his twenty-first birthday, Hardy walked daily from the rural isolation of his parents' cottage to the centre of Dorchester, a County Town of 'assizes, railways, telegraphs and daily London papers', despite which it remained somewhat a municipality in miniature, still confined within old Roman boundaries. The sharp contrast between two such diverse environments lent a cutting-edge to his subsequent creativity, which was further enhanced by an intense awareness of local history: recent in the form of the fairs that accompanied public hangings and a cholera epidemic; more distant in memories of the Monmouth Rebellion and evidence of human occupation stretching back 5,000 years.

Approach Dorchester in the footsteps of Elizabeth-Jane and Susan Henchard, by walking down Stinsford Hill from the roundabout, for views of the town 'compact as a box of dominoes'. At Grey's Bridge, take the riverside path to your right for a fine prospect of the town across the watermeadows. Stop at Ten Hatches Hole, which Henchard 'was intending to make his death-bed' until shocked out of it by the appearance of a stuffed image of himself floating in the pool, discarded from the skimmity ride. The next stretch of road sadly has little to commend it save the views straight up High East Street.

Dorchester from Ten Hatches Weir: dominated by the (now redundant) prison to the right and the spire of All Saints and the tower of St Peter's to the left.

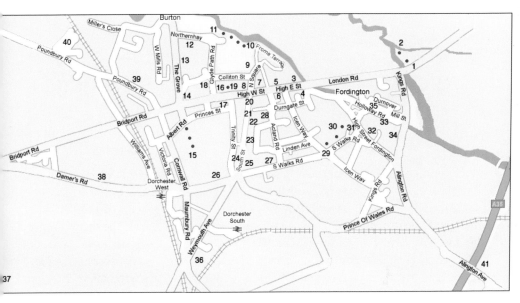

Key to Casterbridge Map

1. Grey's Bridge
2. Ten Hatches Weir
3. The White Hart (site of)
4. Dorford Chapel
5. Three Mariners Inn
6. Phoenix Inn
7. The King's Arms
8. The Bow
9. Casterbridge Gaol
10. Jopp's Cottage (site of)
11. Hangman's Cottage
12. Roman Town House
13. Chalk (Colliton)
14. Hardy Statue
15. West Walks
16. Shire Hall
17. Ship Inn
18. Colliton House
19. Seed & Grain Shop
20. Town Pump
21. Antelope Hotel
22. Henchard's house
23. Napper's Mite
24. The Gorge Café
25. United Church
26. Bowling Alley Walk
27. South Walks
28. Henchard's Corn-store
29. Gallows Hill
30. Salisbury Fields
31. Fordington Vicarage (site of
32. St George's Church)
33. Durnover Barton (site of)
35. Mixen Lane
36. Maumbury Rings
37. (To) Maiden Castle
38. Casterbridge Union
39. The Barracks
40. Poundbury
41. Max Gate.
•••• Footpath

A Circular Walk around Casterbridge (3.5 miles, OS Explorer 15)

Start at Swan Bridge at the bottom of High East Street: entry gate to the Roman town (Durnovaria): there is a car park nearby in Icen Way. To your right, beside the Frome, new houses cover the site of The White Hart, where Hardy was known to pause for a drink and where Sergeant Troy was discovered 'smoking and drinking a steaming mixture from a glass' before his assault on Boldwood's Christmas party. The forecourt of this busy inn was the starting point for carriers' vans, as described in '*A Few Crusted Characters*'. To your left is the original Dorford Baptist Chapel, where Mr Maumbury preached.

Head up High East Street towards the projecting portico of the King's Arms, passing on your right another abandoned inn with adjoining archway: The Three Mariners, rustics

Above left: Last vestiges of the once-proud Phoenix Inn, where at Christmas Jenny danced her final fling with 'The King's-Own Cavalry' in *Far From the Madding Crowd.*

Above right: The King's Arms: here in *The Mayor of Casterbridge* the workfolk watched the Mayor's banquet through the first floor bow window; to the left an archway leads to the stable yard of this once-important coaching stage-post.

meeting place in *The Mayor of Casterbridge*; the subdivided number 16 opposite being the dilapidated remains of the Phoenix Inn (CP28). Pass the redundant All Saint's Church (nature reserve garden, a welcome sanctuary) to number 22, from whose steps the townsfolk gazed in upon Henchard's mayoral banquet across the street. Beyond the King's Arms is the Corn Exchange, the scene of Bathsheba's public appearances as a farmer. Lucetta's house, **High Place Hall** was located on the corner directly opposite the Corn Exchange (One Cornhill), giving her a 'raking view of the market-place'. The few stalls by the pump are the remnants of the great markets which used to occupy the junction of the High Street, Cornhill and Bull-Stake Square. Here stood Gabriel Oak amongst 'two to three hundred blithe and hearty labourers waiting upon Chance' at the Candlemas Fair. Hardy paid for the erection of 'The Bow' sign so that a piece of Dorchester history might not be completely lost.

Turn right into North Square through the narrow entrance, originally arched; here

Beside Hangman's Cottage, the pool 'wherein nameless infants had been used to disappear'; an 'undoubted convenience' of High-Place Hall, reached by 'the steep back lane into town' (Glyde Path).

Henchard's waggon capsized after becoming entangled with Farfrae's, 'the bright heap of new hay' spread across High Street, 'illuminated by the moon's rays'. The now redundant Prison (**Casterbridge Gaol**) stands on the site of a Norman Castle; head down Friary Hill, cross the Frome by the footbridge; the attractive white cottage on your left marks the site '**Jopp's Cottage**'. Turn left along the path beside the river, in the watermeadows on your right, the 'hang crowds' used to gather, including on the morning of 9 August 1856 the impressionable young Thomas Hardy, a spectator at the execution of Martha Browne. Turn left at the T-junction over the bridge; noting the innocuous seeming pool. Bear right past the thatched 'Hangman's Cottage', originally a group of cottages, one of which housed the resident executioner.

Cross the road and follow the path opposite signposted 'Top-of-Town & Roman Town House', the latter soon becomes apparent on your left, excavated in the 1930s, confirming Hardy's observation that 'Casterbridge announced old Rome in every street, alley, and precinct. It looked Roman, bespoke the art of Rome, concealed dead men of Rome'. Follow North Walk to the corner where it turns left into **Chalk** (Colliton) **Walk**; there are fine views behind to the north and west, emphasising the fact that you are standing on a great Roman earthwork, once topped by the walls which enclosed Dorchester on all sides: here Henchard persuaded Farfrae not to emigrate to America but to settle in **Casterbridge**. Approaching Top-o'-Town, you encounter Eric Kennington's somewhat awkward effigy of Hardy, seated within a clump of heathland vegetation. Straight ahead in West Walks

A detail from Eric Kennington's statue of Thomas Hardy near the Top-o'-Town roundabout. Not an easy place to remember the thoughtful man from the heath.

(note fragment of Roman wall) stood the cottage which Henchard rented for Susan 'Newson'; here Farfrae constructed a gigantic tent for dancing by suspending rick-cloths to make a barrel roof at the 'densest point of the avenue of sycamores'.

Return to the northern side of High West Street: the long view downhill from here is as described in the opening paragraph of 'A Changed Man'. Turn left into Glyde Path Road; noting on your right Shire Hall, the original County Hall and once site of the Assizes and Quarter Sessions; Hardy wrote *The Mayor of Casterbridge* whilst lodging in this lane. Colliton House, 17th-century home of the Churchills', was the model for **High Place Hall**, and the setting of the poem 'The Burghers' (CP23), which effectively maps out Hardy's **Casterbridge**. On Elizabeth-Jane's first visit to the house she is unsettled by a leering mask in an arch above a doorway: now preserved in the County Museum library.

Fork right down Colliton Street, then right again into Grey School Passage: on your right is the 'little retail seed and grain shop', which some members of the town council acquired for Henchard after his bankruptcy. Turn left to the Dorset County Museum (1883),

High Place Hall in Lucetta's time: an L-plan stone-faced seventeenth-century house; transposed by Hardy from this site to the corner of South Street.

On Florence's death, Hardy's sister Kate bought Max Gate, donating it to the National Trust to generate income to maintain the Bockhampton Cottage. She also gave the contents of Hardy's study to the County Museum, where the room has been faithfully reconstructed.

the setting for the telling of the tales in *A Group of Noble Dames*. The museum has a permanent Hardy exhibition, including a reconstruction of his Max Gate study. Admire William Barnes' statue in front of St Peter's Church, sole ecclesiastical survivor of the Great Fire of Dorchester (1613). Here at the start of *The Mayor of Casterbridge* Henchard's wife and daughter observe the curfew bell being rung, a custom which continued until 1939; cross the road, turn right into Cornhill past Lloyd's (Hardy's) bank; the stone obelisk marks the remains of the town pump; that original fount of pure water where Mother Cuxsom delivered her eulogy to Susan Henchard.

Pass the residual market stalls to reach the former Antelope Hotel, once Dorchester's principal coaching-inn. Here Henchard waited in vain to hand over Lucetta's billet-doux. Fifty yards further down South Street find Henchard's house, now Barclay's Bank; note the blue plaque also on No. 44, home to Gertrude Bugler, star of the Hardy Players. The ancient clock over the entrance to Napper's Mite almshouses was the cause of Hardy's first appearance in print, whilst working opposite: see plaque above the Gorge Café. Follow South Street to its junction with the Walks; here turn left past the War Memorial

Above: Michael Henchard's house: Pevsner confirms its 'unmistakeable air of superiority, faced with nothing but vitrified headers'. From the open front door Elizabeth-Jane 'could see through the passage to the end of the garden: nearly a quarter of a mile off'.

Left: Blue plaques normally commemorate distinguished real past occupants but such is the pull of Hardy's 'part-dream country' that this fine late eighteenth-century building sports a plaque confirming the status of its fictional inhabitant.

into South Walks, which like the adjoining Salisbury Walk are composed of horse chestnut, forming an enchanting canopy in early May. Charles Street on your left is Hardy's '**Back Street**' where Abel Whittle lived; the projecting stone barn at the further end of Charles Street marks the current end of Henchard's property, which in the text extended as far as Acland Road.

Follow South Walks onward to Gallows Hill, cross Icen Way and continue ahead into Salisbury Fields; to your left the 'deserted avenue of chestnuts' up which Fanny Robin struggled, supported by the dog, on her way to the Union Workhouse. Follow the southern boundary of the fields (**Durnover Hill**) noting the beacon and fine views behind of the prison and churches; over the wall on your right in the alleyway ahead stood Fordington Vicarage, home of Revd Henry Moule, the inspiration for Maumbury in 'A Changed Man' and the model for Revd Clare in *Tess*. Head towards Fordington Green, a tree-lined oasis dominated by St George's; pass left behind the church and across the gate into the cemetery. Here Elizabeth-Jane visiting her mother's grave encountered Lucetta about the same purpose; below them stood **Durnover Barton**, where Elizabeth-Jane and Farfrae met by anonymous invitation.

Absorb the extensive views across **Durnover Moor** towards Stinsford Church with **Egdon** rising behind; follow the path down to King's Road and turn left to cross the Frome by the now-redundant Standfast Bridge. To the left of **Durnover Mill** rises Holloway Row, still containing some 19th-century terraced cottages: as close as you can get now to the feel of that 'Adullam of all the surrounding villages', Hardy's **Mixen Lane**; here in Cuckolds' Row the 1854 Cholera epidemic started. Even at the time of writing *The Mayor*

Mixen Lane (1880): 'A white apron is suspicious vesture in situations where spotlessness is difficult; moreover, the industry and cleanliness which the white apron expressed were belied by the postures and gaits of the women who wore it.' *The Mayor of Casterbridge.*

Maiden Castle: 'at one's every step forward Mai-Dun rises higher against the south sky, with an obtrusive personality that compels the senses to regard it and consider.'

of Casterbridge (1885), Hardy admits that it was 'now in great part pulled down'. Follow Mill Street, no longer 'an altar to disease' but a pleasant lane bordered by one or two Victorian cottages, narrowing down into a shady path beside the Frome, back to your starting point, Swan Bridge.

Ancient Earthworks

Maumbury Rings (CP27) where Henchard first re-encounters Susan, Lucetta comes to beg the return of her letters and Henchard spies upon Farfrae and Elizabeth-Jane. At his meeting with Susan, the mayor enters 'by the south path', where in March 1705 the eighteen-year-old Mary Channing was half-strangled and then burnt at the stake in front of 10,000 spectators. Hardy described this terrible event in *The Mayor of Casterbridge*, in 'The Mock Wife' (CP728) and in *The Times* of October 9 1908: an article commissioned because archaeological excavations had just revealed Maumbury to be a Neolithic hill-top henge, adapted by the Romans as an amphitheatre, modified by the Parliamentarians as a gun emplacement, then becoming the town gallows. The rings retain their historical role as the town's major site of public assembly for events of both national and local importance.

Mai-Dun (Maiden Castle), the largest Iron Age hillfort in Europe, dominates the skyline to the south of the town; extending over half-a-mile in length and enclosing within its five miles of multiple ramparts an area of 47 acres. 'A Tryst in an Ancient Earthwork' is a

Max Gate. Designed by Hardy and his home from 1885 until his death. It was here he wrote both *Tess of the d'Urbervilles* and *Jude the Obscure*.

comprehensive, evocative portrait of Maiden Castle as explored on a stormy winter night; the earthwork a metaphor for the larger world in its state of permanent conflict, motion, change and decay.

Max Gate

Max Gate, Hardy's home from 29 June 1885 until he died there on 11 January 1928, is a typical brick villa of the 1880s, designed by Hardy to be comfortable and functional; built by his brother and father on an exposed hill-top site, a former Roman and Bronze Age burial-ground. Hardy planted 'some two or three thousand small trees, mostly Austrian Pines' and beech as a screen 'both from winds, and eyes that tease'. The National Trust now open the house to the public for most of the year, nearly all the rooms can be inspected and the full atmosphere of house and garden absorbed as you sit on 'The Garden Seat' (CP518) or visit the Pets' Cemetery, last resting place of Snowdove (CP619), Wessex (CPs776,907) and Kitsey (CP329). Max Gate resonates with Hardy's poetry from the well-known 'An August Midnight' (CP113), 'The Going' (CP277), and 'The Spell of the Rose' (CP295), to a whole host of poems concerning marriage, memory, moonlight and mortality (CPs164, 259, 274, 283, 286, 373, 413, 430, 435, 446, 457, 482, 483, 517, 691). Do visit: you will not be disappointed!

FIVE

The Piddle & the Frome

These two parallel rivers carve an eastward path through **Egdon Heath**, feeding the water-meadows, ancient villages and market towns which constitute the core landscape of Hardy's most successful fiction. Both can easily be explored by car, but they also offer a wonderful variety of walks.

The Piddle Valley (A35: Old Route)   *Far from the Madding Crowd*

Leave Dorchester by the London Road up Stinsford Hill, passing Fanny Robin's fourth and third milestones: bear left at the start of the dual carriageway following the old coach road up Yellowham Hill; here Bathsheba and Troy encountered Fanny Robin on her last journey to the Union (the Workhouse) and in Yalbury Wood Joseph Poorgrass becomes lost on a dark night. (CP704). Beyond the wood, the road descends to a fine 19th-century farmhouse: **Roy-Town**, 'a roadside hamlet on the old western turnpike road': opposite stood that once-important coaching-inn, The Buck's Head; reduced now to an outhouse, sheltering livestock. Here Poorgrass, becalmed in autumn fog with his melancholy burden ,indulges in 'very pretty drinking' until afflicted by 'a multiplying eye'; and Gabriel Oak approaching **Weatherbury** crept into the back of a wagon to sleep. The railways came, the coaches went and so did the inn, the road was quiet; the motorcar came, the road was noisy and busy; the bypass came and **Roy-town** slumbers once more. 'So do flux and reflux; the rhythm of change; alternate and persist in everything under the sky'.

Puddletown. This is Hardy's **Weatherbury** – a thriving small market town in the 19th century; the one best known to Hardy during his childhood: a mere 2½-miles across **Egdon** whilst Dorchester was 3¼-miles away. Hardy had ten cousins in Puddletown: the children of his mother's sisters Maria Sparks and Mary Antell. Entering Puddletown on the old main road, the large grey house behind a high wall on the left at the traffic-lights marks the location for **Weatherbury Upper Farm**, but the building described had, as Hardy admitted, 'taken a witch's ride of a mile or more from its actual position'.

Turn down Mill Street and then right into the Square, which has changed little in the last 150-years. In Back Street (to left of thatched house with pillars), the irregular single-storey building called the Bread Oven incorporates the remains of **Warren's Malthouse**.

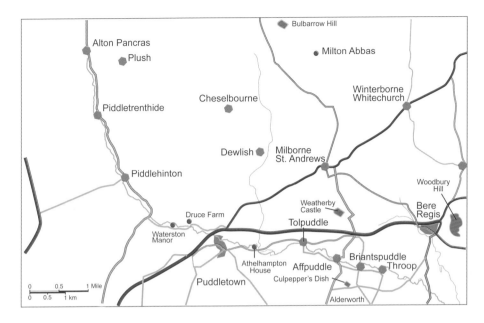

The entrance porch to the church still contains the narrow benches on which Sergeant Troy spent an uncomfortable night as rain spouting from the 'gurgoyle' washed the plants away from Fanny's grave. The gargoyle remains on the north-west angle of the tower with its output carefully piped away. Ancient yews still populate the corner where Fanny was buried; beyond it find the headstone to Hardy's Sparks aunt and uncle (parents of Tryphena); their grave lies beneath the new church hall.

Puddletown church thankfully escaped Victorian restoration; in the box pew left of the gallery stairs find the carved **HENERY**: the variant spelling insisted upon by Henery Fray. Admire the knightly tombs, especially the figure of Sir William Martyn of

Puddletown church escaped the heavy hand of the Victorian restorers; its interior largely unaltered from the refurbishment of 1634-7, retaining its oak box pews, pulpit, open chancel screen and west end gallery: exemplifying Stinsford's loss.

Waterston Manor (**Weatherbury Upper Farm**): Bathsheba's home. Hardy gives a lengthy description of 'this hoary building' in chapter 9 of *Far from the Madding Crowd*.

Athelhampton House (**Athelhall**): open to the public throughout the summer, built by Sir William Martyn, Lord Mayor of London in 1493 and extended by his descendants.

Druce Farm (**Little Weatherbury**): Boldwood's home.

Athelhampton (nose eroded) commemorated in 'The Children and Sir Nameless' (CP584). Hardy's description of the d'Urberville tombs at **Kingsbere** (Bere Regis), where Alec reclined pretending to be an effigy, owes much to Puddletown Church, setting also of 'The Christening' (CP214), a satire on both marriage and Christianity.

In creating **Weatherbury**, Hardy performed a telescopic contraction of the countryside around Puddletown. Waterston Manor, the model for Bathsheba's farmhouse, lies two miles distant and Boldwood's **Little Weatherbury Farm** over a mile away; now isolated from the village by that thundering divider, the bypass. A bridleway leads upstream to Druce and Waterston, or take The Moor past the Blue Vinny (formerly The Cat, a thatched inn which burnt down), crossing the bypass to reach Druce. Continue a mile further through the Piddle watermeadows to Waterston; admire the house through the trees; the garden is occasionally open to the public in the summer. Pevsner considers Waterston to be 'the most charming of 17th-century Dorset manor houses'.

Continue upstream beside the Piddle (right at T-junction) to reach first Piddlehinton (**Lower Longpuddle**) and then Piddletrenthide (**Upper Longpuddle**) along the route taken by Burthen's carrier's van in 'A Few Crusted Characters'. **Upper Longpuddle** Church is the setting of 'Absentmindedness in a Parish Choir'. Beyond **Longpuddle** lies Alton Pancras, the source of the Piddle, and the village of Plush; Tess Durbeyfield's **Flintcomb Ash**. Turn left at Higher Waterston for **Slyre's Lane** (CP152); follow this uphill to Waterston Ridge and take the bridleway right to Fiddler's Green, the ruined original of Shepherd Fennel's Cottage ('The Three Strangers').

Manor Farm, below Weatherbury Castle. Hardy confirmed that *Two on a Tower* was based on 'two real spots in the part of the country specified, each of which has a column standing upon it.'

East from Puddletown: follow the old High Road to Athelhampton, one of the finest houses in Wessex: famous for its great hall, musician's gallery, vast oriel window and superb gardens. Hardy was familiar with this house, where his father had worked as a stonemason. **Endelstow House** in *A Pair of Blue Eyes* is based upon Athelhampton rather than its local model, Lanhydrock (see page 53). In 'The Waiting Supper', Christine and Nicholas dance together on the lawn at **Athelhall**, whilst attending a Christening party (CP124). Beyond Athelhampton is Tolpuddle: **Tolchurch** in *Desperate Remedies* where Owen superintends the church restoration; his lodging being the Manor House, below the church on the Affpuddle road. Beyond Affpuddle lies Briantspuddle, a delightful sleepy mossy thatched village, named after Brianus-de-Thorbeville, a 13th-century lord-of-the-manor; beyond this a sharp, left turn marks Throop Corner where Venn spies Eustacia and Wildeve, returning together from the 'Gipsying'.

Cross over the Piddle, under the bypass and follow the narrow lane uphill passing on your left a wooded hillfort, Weatherby Castle, its monument obscured by trees. This is one of the models for *Two on a Tower*: the other being at Charborough, clearly visible on the skyline near Red Post heading east on the A31. Welland House is similarly an amalgam of the decaying manor house beside the church in Milborne St Andrew (**Millpond-St-Jude**) and the far grander Charborough Park (behind long brick wall on A31). The park, 'the most splendid in Dorset' (Pevsner) is occasionally open to the public when you can inspect the tower and the 'long, low front of the Great House'.

From Milborne, take Roke Road to Bere Regis, that 'little one-eyed blinking sort of place'; 'the half-dead townlet' where the d'Urbervilles had resided 'for full five-hundred-years'. To the right of the church door Joan Durbeyfield installed the old four-post bedstead. Inside inspect the Turberville window: memorial to the Norman knights, on whom Hardy based his d'Urbervilles. Admire the nave roof, adorned with full-length figures of the twelve apostles, portrayed as 15th-century Dorset men. To the east of the church a rough

Bere Regis Church, the Turberville window. 'Over the tester of the bedstead was a beautiful traceried window, of many lights, its date being fifteenth century'.

paddock marks the site of the Turberville mansion, demolished in 1832, apart from one wall incorporated into the surviving cottages.

Behind, rises Woodbury Hill, from 1267 until 1914 the site of an annual fair: the **Greenhill Fair** of *Far from the Madding Crowd*, to which crowds flocked to see 'The Royal Hippodrome Performance of Turpin's Ride to York' and other associated marvels.

The Frome: (A 352)

Below Dorchester, the Frome opens out into the **Valley of the Great Dairies**, first observed by Tess standing on **Rainbarrow** 'on a thyme-scented, bird-singing morning in May' as 'the verdant plain so well watered by the Var or Froom', where 'milk and butter grew to rankness'. By car, pass Max Gate on the A352 but then bear left (three times),

Stafford House: setting of the most successful love story in Hardy's fiction, for Christine and Nicholas never come together remaining joyfully separate 'in the days of our vanity.'

pausing at the third junction to admire the magnificent 'mullioned and transomed' Elizabethan Stafford House (**Froom-Everard House**) home to Christine Everard in 'The Waiting Supper'. Head across the watermeadows to Lower Bockhampton along the (then) flooded lane where Angel carried the three milkmaids. Bear right at Bockhampton Cross, passing the tree-enshrouded Heedless William's Pond; as the Tincleton Road descends, **Rainbarrow** towers above you to the left and Norris Mill Farm, the original of **Talbothays**

Norris Mill Farm as it stood when Tess fell in love with Angel. Hardy confirmed Windle's opinion that 'Norris Mill Farm, by situation and general characters, has the best right to be considered as the original for **Talbothays**'.

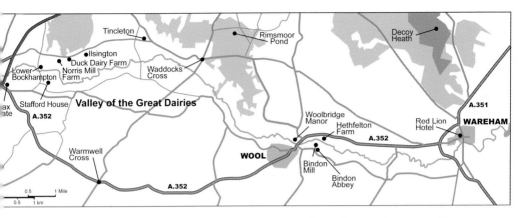

is on your right: explore the footpaths which pass through the farmyard, where sadly none of the original farm buildings survive.

Below Norris Mill is Duck Dairy Farm, the site of Wildeve's **Quiet Woman Inn**. The original building, known as 'The Travellers' Rest' (CP563) has been demolished but it is easy to envisage Eustacia standing above alone on the barrow. Beyond the Quiet Woman,

Wellbridge Manor (Wool Manor) viewed from 'the great Elizabethan bridge': 'once portion of a fine manorial residence, seat of a d'Urberville, but since its partial demolition a farmhouse.'

the extensive woods to the right conceal **Shadwater Weir** (Nine-Hatches, Islington) where Eustacia and Wildeve drown on a stormy November night. The opening passages of *The Return of the Native* describe the road beyond to Tincleton. At Waddock Cross the wooded heath ahead encloses **Alderworth** (Clym Yeobright's marital home), Rimsmoor Pond and Okers Pool; turn right to regain the A352 at Warmwell Cross, site of the ambush of the Revenue men in 'The Distracted Preacher', the road then passes Overmoigne, crossing the smugglers' routes to the coast at **Lulwind** (Lulworth Cove) and Burning Cliff.

Wellbridge

The rivulets, streams and winterbournes which nourish the great dairies of the valley unite in the Frome before reaching Wool; forming the most popular illustration of Hardy's landscape: **Wellbridge Manor** and bridge viewed from across the river. Although Wool has become a small town, the ancestral home of the Turbervilles remains isolated in the riverside flats, the hag-like profiles faded into brown obscurity and the traffic diverted away. Hardy's contracting kaleidoscope was at work here for the mill which Angel went to study and the semi-submerged tomb in the ruins of Bindon Abbey where the sleep-walking Clare laid his fallen 'angel' to rest lie over a mile from the mansion. Neither Abbey (abolished 1539) nor mill are open to the public but the mill is clearly visible from the train. On **Egdon**, due north of the mill stands Hethfelton: the **Holmstoke** of Farmer Lodge. A few miles downstream from Bindon, the rivers Frome and Piddle converge on the ancient Saxon walled-town of **Anglebury** (Wareham), where Thomasin and Wildeve failed to marry at the start of *The Return of the Native*. Here Ethelberta, sets off from 'The Red Lion', 'an old and well-appointed inn', to explore the adjoining Decoy Heath.

'Those horrid women!' One of the two (now badly degraded) Turberville 'portraits on panels built into the masonry' in Wool Manor which so frightened Tess.

SIX

West of Wessex

On Monday 7 March 1870, Hardy rose at 4am and walked to Dorchester West Station to undertake a complex railway journey which eventually deposited him in Cornwall at Launceston Station at 4.03 pm. Three hours later he arrived at St Juliot Rectory, to be 'received by a young lady in brown', Emma Gifford, the vicar's sister-in-law. It was the start of a three-day visit, carefully documented in the diaries of both parties, for by the time Tom departed at dawn on Friday 11 March, he and Emma were undoubtedly in love. (CPs254/360).

For Hardy, 'this wild weird western shore' (CP291) was the most special of all landscapes; here he fell in love with the most influential woman in his life; after her death he returned and fell in love with her and the landscape all over again, in the process generating the poems of 1912-13, the most profound sequence of poems charting love and loss in the English language. Although Hardy denied the possibility of any autobiographical content in his fiction, *A Pair of Blue Eyes* is a close retelling of his four year courtship of Emma Gifford. Fortunately, St Juliot, the Valency Valley, Boscastle Harbour and the wild clifftops are virtually unchanged in the 145 years since Hardy first set foot on them: it is therefore possible to follow directly in the footsteps of Thomas and Emma, Stephen and Elfride.

Pentargon Bay: the precipitate black 'Cliff without a Name' straight ahead; the stream to the right. This is the southern end of Beeny.

Emma Gifford and Thomas Hardy at the time of their first meeting, when both were twenty-nine.

The Walk (8 miles, OS Explorer 111)

Although the full walk is eight miles long, it is easy to divide it into smaller sections – see footpaths on OS map; St Juliot church and Beeny, midway points of the walk, can readily be reached by car.

Start from Boscastle, where there is a capacious village centre car park; cross the Valency River by the road bridge, noting the 'overshot watermill' and the Wellington Hotel, where Hardy stayed on his visit in March 1913. A climb up the Old Road straight ahead leads to the composition of one of his greatest poems 'At Castle Boterel' (CP292). Follow the riverbank towards the sea, turning right up the waymarked coastal path just beyond the Visitor Centre. As you climb the steep path up Penally Hill, there are fine views over the harbour, which extend into a southerly panorama with Forrabury Church prominent; it's isolated hilltop position against 'the serene impassive sea', used by Hardy as the setting for **West Endelstow** Church. The view soon switches northward as you head around the cliff edge towards Pentargon Bay. The next two miles of coastal path form the magical heartland of both A Pair of Blue Eyes and 'The Poems of 1912-13', in particular the four poems which immediately precede 'At Castle Boterel' (CPs288-291). The sheer black cliff

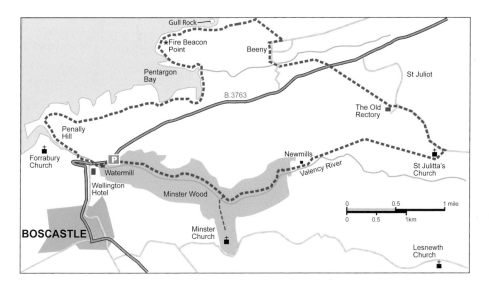

Boscastle Harbour: a mixture of natural haven, medieval breakwater and reconstructed 16th century jetty.

The Old Rectory, St. Juliot, on a March morning, as encountered by Hardy in 1870. It remains the 'little paradise of flowers and trees' described in *A Pair of Blue Eyes*.

ahead, which forms the northern boundary of Pentargon Bay is Hardy's 'Cliff without a name', the scene of Knight's foolish experiment with his hat, which left him suspended over the cliff edge, confronting the fossil of a trilobite; like himself, seemingly, frozen in death. Landslides have destroyed the path used by Hardy to the beach and caves; today accessible only by boat.

After rounding the summit of the 'Cliff without a Name' the narrow path slowly ascends along the edge of Beeny to Fire Beacon Point. Hardy first visited here on 10 March 1870, walking beside Emma who was mounted on her 'beloved Fanny': Emma was to become Elfride and later 'The Phantom Horsewoman' (CP294). Revisiting Beeny one wet Monday in August 1870, Emma remarked that 'It never looks like summer here'; this became the opening line of a poem dated 8/3/13 (CP456). On that rainy day Hardy sketched Beeny: his drawing shows Gull Rock and Buckator; on a clear day there are magnificent views along the coast south to Pentire and north to Hartland Point. Follow the path ahead along the edge of the next three fields, cross the fourth stile to reach a cliff edge seat facing Gull Rock and Buckator, which appears in *A Pair of Blue Eyes* as **Windy Beak**, 'the second cliff in height along that coast' and 'the cliff to which Elfride had ridden with Stephen Smith, on a well-remembered morning of his summer visit'. Here was the seat where Elfride lost an ear-ring whilst kissing Smith, only to find it again whilst kissing Knight.

Cross back over the stile and turn left inland, following the path to the road; turn right along the lane downhill and across Emma's Pentargon-bound stream. From here take the footpath straight ahead to reach and cross straight over the main Boscastle Road: follow this path, which is the exact route followed by Emma and Thomas 145 years ago, straight ahead across five fields via ancient stiles to reach the Rectory of St Juliot. The Old Rectory, built in 1847, remains virtually unchanged from that windy March night in 1870 when Emma first greeted Hardy at the front door. It is currently an award-winning environmentally-friendly bed-and-breakfast, steeped in Hardyan details and run by the most congenial and informative hosts. A stay there is a must for any true Hardy enthusiast. More of Hardy's poems are associated with the Old Rectory than with any other single building (at least 35), particularly 'In Time of 'The Breaking of Nations'' (CP500), written in the darkest days of World War I, 'She Opened the Door' (CP740), 'The Frozen Greenhouse' (CP706) and 'A Dream or No' (CP288).

From the Rectory, the narrow grass-embossed lane gently curves down towards the 'pinnacled tower' of St Julitta's. Admire the magical setting of this typical Cornish churchyard, in spring asparkle with snowdrops and daffodils; an integral part of the wild

The view from the garden seat where Hardy and Emma read Tennyson's 'In Time of 'The Breaking of Nations' in August 1870 in the midst of the Franco-Prussian War as a ploughman tilled the fields on the hillside opposite the rectory.

St Julitta's Church. In 1870 the tower was collapsing and apart from the south aisle and porch, the church was beyond salvation. The caption under the illustration reads: 'St Juliot Church, Cornwall - Before Restoration in 1870. From a Water-colour drawing by Miss Emma Gifford, afterwards Mrs Thomas Hardy'.

hillside. Display boards just inside the door give a detailed history of Hardy's involvement with the church; note the three memorial tablets on the north wall: the first to Cadell Holder, Hardy's brother-in-law, the second erected by Hardy in memory of Emma; the third to Hardy himself, erroneously stating that he 'is buried in Westminster Abbey'. (CPs359/371/598/617/671).

From the church door, take the path straight ahead over the slate stile beside the Celtic cross into the field, bear half-right and follow the clearly waymarked route towards the wooded Valency Valley, of which there are fine views ahead as it curves down to the sea. Soon you cross at right-angles the path running from the Old Rectory to Lesnewth Church, **East Endelstow** of *A Pair of Blue Eyes*. Next, the isolated stone house on your right is probably Widow Jethway's cottage, merged in the text by Hardy with ruined Penventon Cottage, encountered on your left in the wood. Climb uphill through the trees, then descend to New Mills, where the second cottage on your left is Stephen Smith's parental home. Now a tributary stream joins the Valency, increasing the velocity of the river and producing a series of small waterfalls; the setting of the stream-side picnic in August 1870, during which a drinking-glass slipped from Emma's hand and was lost ('Under the Waterfall' CPs276/646). The drinking-glass is perhaps still wedged under a boulder, awaiting discovery, although more likely it has long-since disintegrated or been swept out to sea in the periodical flash floods which devastate this steep valley. This area enchanted Knight in *A Pair of Blue Eyes*: 'Elfride, I never saw such a sight!' he exclaimed. 'The hazels overhang the river's course in a perfect arch, and the floor is beautifully paved.'

Hardy sketched Emma, all breast and bottom, as she knelt beside the brook, later recalling these 'Best Times' (CP646). Note the footbridge to Minster: a diversion to this mystic church set deep in a woody glade is well-worth the effort. Otherwise follow the stream back to **Castle Boterel**.

Some Recollections

Hardy's 'Poems of 1912-13' owe a significant debt to Emma's *Recollections*, written in her attic eyrie at Max Gate during 1911, recalling those far-off days of their courtship. Visiting 'out-of-season', you can experience this coast much as Hardy first saw it in March 1870. A seven-mile walk along the coastal path south-west from Boscastle to Trebarwith takes in the Rocky Valley, Bossiney and Tintagel, some beautiful coastal scenery and a fair chance of spotting seals, basking sharks and plentiful seabirds. Alternatively follow Elfride and Knight by taking a drive 'along a road by neutral green hills, upon which hedgerows lay trailing like ropes on a quay to Barwith Strand' (B3263). Divert to Tintagel: the island is an enchanting magical place: the essence of 'that wild weird western shore' and as **Castel Dyntagell**, the setting of *The Famous Tragedy of the Queen of Cornwall*, written in memory of that 'Iseult of my own', the Emma of 'I found Her Out There' (CP281). The coastal path back from Trebarwith affords beautiful views back towards 'Dundagel's famed head'; deviate from the path to inspect St Merteriana's Church in isolated splendour; where

Widow Jethway's cottage: 'some way down the valley, and under a row of scrubby oaks . . . absolutely alone'.

'Sometimes we all drove to Tintagel and Trebarwith Strand where donkeys were employed to carry seaweed to the farmers; Strangles Beach also, Bossiney, Bude and other places on the coast. Lovely drives they were with sea-views all along.' (Emma's *Recollections*).

Hardy attended a service on his last visit to Cornwall with Florence in September 1916.

'The Interloper' (CP432) describes Hardy's drive with Emma and her sister Helen 'to Boscastle, Tintagel and Penpethy slate-quarries with a view to the church roofing' in March 1870, accompanied on this drive by 'another, whom I like not to be there': this interloper being the Gifford's hereditary tendency to mental instability. The Penpethy slate-quarries are still being worked and welcome visitors. At nearby Trewarmett, a narrow lane leads steeply down to Trebarwith Strand (wise to consult the tide-tables before visiting) where at the right moment the beautiful bay will burst upon you, very much as described by Hardy in *A Pair of Blue Eyes*.

Lanhydrock, a National Trust property, 17 miles south-east of St Juliot, is the original for **Endelstow House**; externally matching the text of *A Pair of Blue Eyes* but with much of detail coming from Athelhampton; the depiction of the opening of the Luxellian family vault being based upon the O'Brien's tomb at Stinsford.

Somerset

A Laodicean, Hardy's Somerset novel, is based ostensibly at Dunster but with significant borrowings from Corfe Castle near Swanage. A visit to Dunster is well-worthwhile and can be taken as part of a tour through western Wessex, heading from **Casterbridge** to **Narrobourne**, **Ivell**, **Ivelchester**, **Glaston**, Sedgemoor, **Wylls-Neck**, **Cliff Martin**

and **Castle Boterel**. Dunster Castle, a National Trust property, retains a fairy-tale magic, especially in distant view as first glimpsed from the approaching A358; with a well-preserved Baptist Chapel by the north gate, matching Hardy's description. Whilst both Dunster and Corfe still boast a working steam railway, one must not underestimate the phallic significance of the train thrusting through the Powers' Tunnel in Hardy's 'Story of Today', neither railway line has a single tunnel. See also 'A Trampwoman's Tragedy' (CP153).

The Cornish National Trust house, Lanhydrock, is the model for **Endelstow House** in *A Pair of Blue Eyes*.

SEVEN

The Jurassic Coast

Hardy's **Port Bredy**, the setting of 'Fellow-Townsmen' is a combination of Bridport and West Bay: of note in East Street are the 18th-century Town Hall, Black Bull Hotel, United Church and nearby King Street, where Downe lived. Follow South Street past St Mary's Church where Downe and Lucy, and Farfrae and Lucetta were married. Beyond the roundabout, bungalows (Wanderwell) cover the knoll on which 'Chateau Ringdale' was constructed: to reach West Bay and the thatched 'Harbour Inn'. From here the coastal road leads east to Weymouth passing the medieval Abbey Barn at Abbotsbury, a model for Bathsheba's shearing barn. Beside the road junction in nearby Portesham still stands the unchanged Manor, home of Nelson's flag captain at Trafalgar, Admiral Hardy, where Bob Loveday volunteered for naval service.

Comer's Hill, **Port-Bredy**: where 'The shepherd on the east hill could shout out lambing intelligence to the shepherd on the west hill, over the intervening town chimneys.'

West Bay, scene of Emily Downe's drowning: 'the vertical cliff coloured a burning orange by the sunlight'; the glorious start of the coastal footpath to **Budmouth**.

The Tithe Barn, Abbotsbury, A watercolour of 1795 by Thomas Girtin, and a good idea of what it may have looked like when Hardy used it as a model for Bathsheba's shearing barn in *Far from the Madding Crowd* (a similar claim is made for the the Tithe Barn at Cerne Abbas).

A Weymouth walk with Hardy (Two miles, OS Explorer 15)

Starting from the Railway Station yard, head for the Esplanade, turn left along Royal Crescent past The Langham Hotel (formerly The Belvidere where Miss Aldclyffe interviewed Cytherea in *Desperate Remedies*), and Hotel Prince Regent to cross the road to the pier bandstand. Hardy stood here in April 1869, following an interview with the architect Crickmay, 'facing the beautiful sunlit bay' listening to the band playing a Strauss Waltz. (CP447). Whilst living in Weymouth Hardy swam in the mornings from the shingle beach north of the bandstand and rowed in the Bay in the evenings. Retrace your steps along the front with views ahead of the harbour and Portland behind, topped by the Verne. Throughout Hardy's fiction, if characters travel abroad, they invariably depart from **Budmouth**. Beyond the Jubilee Clock, stands the rebuilt Royal Hotel, former Assembly Rooms where George III and his daughters danced, a red cord separating the royals from the townsfolk. Cross over to the statue of King George and his adjoining bathing-machine. Turn back down Westham Road, then right and left into Wooperton Street; note the plaque on number 3 where Hardy lodged in 1869-71.

Continue towards Westham Bridge, bearing left along the quayside path beside the marina to reach and cross 'The Harbour Bridge' (CPs304,539,742) into Weymouth proper; continue along the quayside, noting the boat trips on offer. Bear first-right up Trinity Street, opposite Hope Congregational Chapel stands an early 17th-century house (see plaque), Hardy's **Old Rooms Inn**, drinking place in *The Dynasts* where boatmen and burghers discuss Nelson's long journey back to England, his body preserved 'in a case

'At a Seaside Town in 1869': The boats, the sands, the esplanade,/ The laughing crowd;/ Light-hearted, loud// The keen sea-salts,/ The band, the Morgenblatter Waltz' (CP447).

'Immediately the King entered the water, a deafening noise burst forth, the musicians striking up 'God save the King, a performance tolerated rather than desired by that dripping monarch.' *The Trumpet Major*.

View from Harbour Bridge: 'One pairing is as good as another/ Where all is venture! Take each other,/ And scrap the oaths that you have aforetime made'. 'The Contretemps' (CP 539).

of sperrits' but 'the grog ran short so they broached the Adm'll'. Continue past the old cottages, left across the top end of Hope Square and straight on up the path ahead between walls and across Horsford Street to reach Nothe Gardens. Pause to breathe in the scenery. In the cove below Christoph waited with the boat he had stolen to rendezvous with 'The Melancholy Hussar of the German Legion'. (Divert one mile south along coastal path to find the ruins of **Henry VIII's Castle**).

Otherwise, turn left, following the seaward path, curving up across the greensward above Nothe Fort to the upper (wooded) path above Barrack Road, from where there are fine views across **Budmouth** Harbour towards the chalk depiction of King George on his charger; turn right down to the quayside for the rowing boat ferry across the harbour. Head straight to the beach and Esplanade, for this is the bright, lively seaside resort which throughout Hardy's writings appears the antithesis to sombre lonely **Egdon**: the **Budmouth** of the 'Hussar's Song' from *The Dynasts*:

When we lay where Budmouth Beach is,
O, the girls were fresh as peaches,
With their tall and tossing figures
And their eyes of blue and brown! (CP930)

Many other poems recall Hardy's life as a young man in Weymouth (CPs173,174,182, 341,660,682,688). Turn away from the waterfront across the road: the shop on the corner of Bond Street marks the site of the Theatre Royal, visited by George III; here Matilda Johnson acts in *The Trumpet-Major*. Beyond find Gloucester Lodge, George III's regular summer residence (see plaque) (CP915).

Looking west along Chesil Beach and Portland Harbour. In the foreground, **The Street of the Wells** where stand 'the houses above houses, one man's doorstep rising behind his neighbour's chimney.'

Portland

In *The Well-Beloved* Hardy called Portland **The Isle of Slingers**, describing it as the 'peninsula carved by Time out of a single stone'.

By foot, follow the Coastal Path along Chesil Beach to the 'Gibraltar of Wessex', then like Pierston in *The Well-Beloved*, 'a laborious clamber' to 'reach the top'. By car, park in New Ground (behind Heights Hotel). The knoll just south of the car park is Hardy's **Top-o'-Hill**, with superb views over Chesil Beach and Portland Harbour towards West Bay and Lyme Regis..

The Isle of Slingers Walk (9 miles, OS Explorer 15)

Although the full Portland coastal walk is nine miles long, it is easy to split it into smaller segments – see the OS map; by car the walk can be divided into four sections by stopping at the car parks at Church Hope, Portland Bill and St George's Church, Reforne.

Follow the footpath north beside the road (New Ground) to the entrance to Verne Prison, approached by a 'drawbridge' over a deep moat. Two of Hardy's first cousins were warders at the Prison. Avice II, who suffers from Pierston's susceptibility to multiple simultaneous Well-Beloveds, takes in washing for the fortress, where a soldier has caught her eye: this leads to a typical Hardyan scene in which Pierston is watching Avice watch the soldier. Follow the track past the Verne entrance, curving southward to pass to the seaward site of The Grove; once clear of this second prison, there are fine views east along the Jurassic Coast to St Aldhelm's Head. Inland is Yeoman's Quarry, now in part a nature reserve. Portland Stone has been quarried since Roman times; peaking in the late 19th century when it became the premium material for public buildings throughout Great Britain.

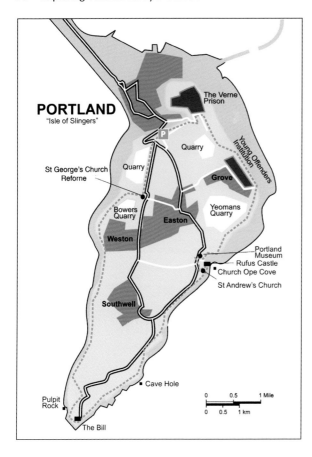

Approaching Church Ope Cove turn right away from the coast under the Archway of Red King's Castle, follow this lane to **Avice's Cottage** (now the Portland Museum), where the twenty-year-old Pierston first re-encounters the Avice I and twenty years later spies on Ann-Avice. Bear left back towards the sea beside **Sylvania Castle**, rented by Pierston during the summer of his courtship of Ann-Avice. The wooded footpath leads into the churchyard containing the remains of the fourteenth-century St Andrew's church; Pierston and Avice wander in darkness 'to the old Hope Churchyard, which lay in a ravine formed by a landslip ages ago.'

Head down towards the beach, then bear right up the coastal path; admire secluded Church Ope Cove (**Hope Cove**), the only beach on Portland; frequently visited in *The Well-Beloved*, and by Anne Garland in *The Trumpet-Major*. The path climbs through Southwell Landslip and then follows the road for about 300 yards before returning down a track to the cliff-edge, passing Cheyne House, Pierston's parental home, subsequently occupied by Avice III. Head towards Portland Bill (**The Beal**), looking out for 'the treacherous cavern known as Cave Hole, into which the sea roared and splashed'. Anne Garland followed 'the central track' down the island to reach the solitude of 'the wild, herbless, weather-worn promontory'. To share this experience, visit on a winter weekday, past the (now automatic) lighthouse to the obelisk projecting above a lunar landscape whilst the waves crash below. Here Anne watches Nelson's HMS *Victory* sail past until the ship is absorbed into the main 'no more than dead fly's wing on a sheet of spider's web'.

Head north from **the Beal**, taking the coastal path up the greensward, passing to the seaward side of the old Upper Lighthouse. The next two miles are straightforward cliff-top

Avice's Cottage: 'which with its quaint and massive stone features of two or three centuries' antiquity.'

walking with fine views over Chesil Beach; on reaching a cliff-top defence converted into a dwelling, take the footpath inland, follow round Bowers Quarries to enter the graveyard of St George's Church, Reforne. This wonderful redundant building, 'the most impressive 18th century church in Dorset', is open on summer afternoons.

St George's Reforne, precariously perched on the edge of a quarry. Pierston 'stretched out his hand upon the rock beside him. It felt warm. That was the island's personal temperature.'

Looking down on Chesil Cover (**Deadman's Bay**) from the West Cliff, Portland.

Pierston, on receiving the news of Avice I's death realises that he loves 'the woman dead and inaccessible as he never loved her in life' and speeds post-haste back to his native peninsula. Late for the funeral: 'He looked southward towards the Beal. The level line of the sea horizon rose above the surface of the isle: against the stretch of water, was defined, in addition to the distant lighthouse, a church with its tower, standing about a quarter of a mile off; Among the graves moved the form of a man clothed in a white sheet; near him moved six men bearing a long box, and two or three persons in black followed'.

Hardy finds his descriptive cinematic best on this magical island; his observation that there are only 'half-a-dozen Christian and surnames in the whole island' is here readily confirmed by an inspection of the gravestones. Follow the path north from the graveyard, curving back to West Cliff, above **Deadman's Bay**; to your right lies Tout Quarry Sculpture Park, Pierston's 21st century successors; ahead the **Street of the Wells**. Follow the path to the derrick, here cross the main road and take the steep path up the bank opposite to the war memorial and New Ground.

The Trumpet-Major and 'The Melancholy Hussar of the German Legion'

Sutton Poyntz with its mill-house and tree-lined duck-laden mill-pond beside is Hardy's **Overcombe**. Several footpaths lead from the village up to East Hill, where King George's troops were encamped: 'at night, it is impossible to avoid hearing, amid the scourings of the wind over the grass-bents and thistles, the old trumpet and bugle calls, the rattle of halters, the guttural syllables of foreign tongues, and songs of the fatherland; for they

George III mounted on his horse: 'Here stretch the downs, high and breezy and green, absolutely unchanged since those eventful days. A plough has never disturbed the turf, and the sod that was uppermost then is uppermost now.'

were mainly regiments of the King's German Legion that slept round the tent-poles hereabout at that time.' The nearby tumulus is 'one of the best view-points in the county' where 'The eye of any observer who cared for such things swept over the wave-washed town, and the bay beyond, and the Isle, with its pebble bank, lying on the sea to the left of these, like a great crouching animal tethered to the mainland. On the extreme east of the marine horizon, St. Aldhelm's Head closed the scene, the sea to the southward of that point glaring like a mirror under the sun.' On adjoining White Horse Hill John Loveday witnesses men 'cutting out a huge picture of the king on horseback'.

An easy track leads west to Bincombe, where an irregular plot to the right marks Dr Grove's house and garden; two small flat stone slabs to the south-east of the graveyard are believed to be the soldiers' graves. The church registers record that 'Matth: Tina (Corpl.), His Majesty's Regmt. of York Hussars, Shot for Desertion, Buried 30 June 1801, aged 22 years. Christoph Bless, His Majesty's Regmt. of York Hussars, Shot for Desertion, Buried June 30th, 1801, aged 22 years.' Further west lies Upwey, where at the junction of Ridgeway and Roman Road the local population gathered to catch a glimpse of the passing Royal carriages. The old road can still be followed, a chalky byway leads through trees down to that 'good inn', The Ship, where Dick rested his horses 'going and coming', and where Dick and Fancy became engaged. Here Hardy also would break his journey, as in the poem 'Great Things', 'Spinning down to Weymouth town by Ridgway thirstily' (CP414).

EIGHT

The Blackmore Vale

For the three principal novels of his mature fiction, Hardy moved north into and then beyond his 'Vale of the Little Dairies', Blackmore. The landscape of *The Woodlanders* is especially problematic because Hardy moved the location of the **Hintocks** further eastward with each revised edition in an attempt to placate the wrath of the Earl of Ilchester, furious that Hardy had put 'a legend of his family' into a book (*A Group of Noble Dames*).

A Woodlanders Walk (seven miles, OS Explorer 117)

Although the full walk is seven miles long, it is easy to divide it into smaller sections – see footpaths on OS map; the villages of Melbury Bubb, Stockwood and Melbury Osmond can readily be reached by car.

Start from The Common at Evershot (NGR ST574045). Head north up Park Lane, bearing right up the bridleway, passing the conifer plantation (listen for their sigh: CP225) towards wooded Bubb Down straight ahead. Pause to look back at **Hintock House** in its wooded glen before cautiously crossing the A37 today sadly far removed from the

Looking north from Bubb Down over the Blackmore Vale. Edred Fitzpiers was 'leaning over a gate on Rub-Down Hill, which opened on the brink of a steep, slanting down directly into Blackmoor Vale.'

'tomb-like stillness' of 'the deserted highway' described at the start of *The Woodlanders*. Follow the bridleway opposite through the wood to reach a gate into a large sloping meadow. At this Blackmore viewpoint, Grace Melbury discovered her infatuated husband 'leaning over a gate on Rub-Down Hill; his attention fixed on the landscape far away'. Dr Fitzpiers disappears 'into the gorgeous autumn landscape' in pursuit of Felice Charmond, to be replaced by Giles Winterbourne who 'looked and smelt like Autumn's very brother'. 'Nature was bountiful,' Grace reflected, 'No sooner had she been starved off by Fitzpiers than another being had arisen out of the earth, ready to hand.'

Follow the bridleway past the Trig Point down into the hamlet of Melbury Bubb, Hardy's **Little Hintock**, where the fine

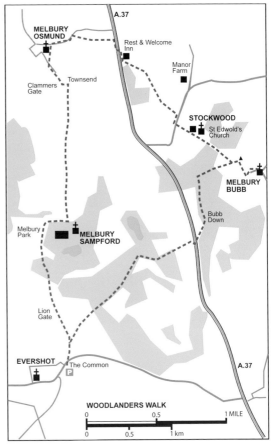

Jacobean Manor House with extensive outbuildings is George Melbury's home; the brick house on the corner of the lane just below the churchyard representing Fitzpiers' lodging. Retrace your steps back to the Trig Point; in the woods above you, the girls sought their marital fortune on 'old Midsummer eve'; here later Grace and Felice spent the night huddled together after becoming hopelessly lost. Follow the track left down a steep slope and through a marshy copse to reach Stockwood, with its farmhouse and tiny St Edwold's church tucked in below the wooded slopes of Bubb Down: another source for **Little Hintock** in Hardy's 'part-real, part-dream' landscape.

Follow the drive to the road, bear right and take the right-hand path, passing Manor Farm, where Jemima Hardy lived after her father's death to reach The Rest and Welcome Inn (the 'little inn' from 'Interlopers at the Knap'). From the pub, cross the A37, taking the footpath opposite and then the lane uphill to Melbury Osmond. Hardy's mother was born in the thatched house on the left at top of hill (No.1); her marriage certificate is on display in Melbury Osmond church (**Great Hintock**), 'standing at the upper part of the village,

Above The Manor House, Melbury Bubb. George Melbury's house, 'once the manorial residence of Little Hintock'.

Below left Monmouth Cottage; birthplace of Hardy's maternal grandmother, Betty Swetman, disowned by her parents for marrying a labourer, George Hand, who sired seven children, then died from drink. See 'Her Late Husband' (CP134).

Below right Melbury Osmund Church, where Hardy's parents were married.

Looking west over the Blackmore Vale from Hambledon Hill.

reached without passing through the street'. Here Grace and Fitzpiers were married and Marty South ultimately is left to eulogise alone over Giles Winterbourne's grave: 'Now, my own, own love, you are mine, and on'y mine; for she has forgot 'ee at last. But I never can forget 'ee; for you was a GOOD man, and did good things!'

Follow the street straight ahead, curving down to the water-splash, passing on your right Manor Farm Cottage (**The Knap**) from the story loosely based upon Hardy's father's nuptial journey to Melbury Osmund. Ahead in Townsend, the fine thatched Monmouth Cottage, home of Hardy's maternal great-grandparents, forms the setting for 'The Duke's Reappearance' (CP134). Follow the lane to Clammers Gate and walk ahead through undulating parkland to soon confront the grand façade of Melbury (Hintock) House, home of the Strangways family since 1500 and of Betty Dornell, 'The First Countess of Wessex'; in the church nearby is a magnificent memorial to Stephen Fox, the Reynard of Hardy's story.

Follow the drive to the right of the house and into the deer park, passing **Tutcombe Bottom**, scene of the barking operations and subsequent storytelling round the fire 'of white witches and black witches'; nearby grows 'Billy Wilkins', over four-hundred years old, described in *The Woodlanders* as 'Great Willy, the largest oak in the wood'. Beyond Stutcombe lies Chelborough, site of Giles' one-storey cottage, of which no trace remains. Glance back over the park and lakes (CP163) before descending via Lion Gate to Evershot Common.

Above Flintcomb Ash: 'The swede-field was a stretch of a hundred odd acres, on the highest ground of the farm, rising above the stony lanchets . . .'

Tess Durbeyfield

The Blackmore Vale, like Wessex itself, appears to be Hardy's own construct; certainly he expanded and redefined its boundaries. **Marlott**: the hamlet of Walton Elm on the Sturminster side of Marnhull was the home of the Durbeyfields. 'Lamb Inn House' on Mowes Lane was **Rolliver's** inn; turn left beyond this, up an anonymous no through road to reach Tess' Cottage. Half a mile further on by road or footpath, at the village centre crossroads stands the

Top left Tess' Cottage: in the novel Hardy offers no description of the cottage exterior; this identification is based upon a visit he made to Marnhull in 1924.

Left Boveridge House, Hardy's model for 'The Slopes', the home of the Stoke-d'Urbervilles: 'Not a manorial home in the ordinary sense' but 'a country-house built for enjoyment pure and simple'.

church of St Gregory, its graveyard well-tended, no sign of Sorrow's grave. Opposite visit the Crown Inn with its 'Pure Drop' bar.

The home of the Stoke-d'Urbervilles is best approached by taking the road from Shaftesbury to Cranborne via Tollard Royal, pausing at Win Green for magnificent views southwards; you then descend the incline (600+ feet) down which Alec drove Tess so wildly, skirting the Larmer Tree Gardens, where Hardy danced on the greensward with Agnes Groves (CP862). Cranborne is **Chaseborough** where the workfolk drank and danced on that fateful Saturday night. The extensive primeval forest east of Cranborne, the scene of Tess's violation by Alec, straddles the boundary between Dorset and Hampshire (CP40): 'a truly venerable tract of forest land, one of the few remaining woodlands in England of undoubted primaeval date, wherein Druidical mistletoe was still found on aged oaks, and where enormous yew-trees, not planted by the hand of man grew as they had grown when they were pollarded for bows.'

A Tess Pilgrimage (from Plush to Beaminster, as a walk, 18 miles, OS Explorer 117)

Hardy gives a clear description of the route taken by Tess in her abortive attempt to obtain financial support from her in-laws. She rose at 3 am because the distance was' fifteen miles each way': in reality it is nearer 18 miles, and in the 21st century is easier enjoyed by car (though there are fine walks along many sections of Tess's route).

That 'starve-acre place' **Flintcomb Ash** is Plush, a hamlet wedged in a crevice between steep downs. By car start from The Brace of Pheasants, head down past Tess' lodging: the cottage projecting awkwardly into the road on the corner below the pub; follow the lane north, to Mappowder, then west to Duntish Cross and along Park Lane to reach the A352 at Middlemarsh; head south past Lyon's Gate to turn right just below High Stoy, where

'Cross-in-Hand, where the stone pillar stands desolate and silent, to mark the site of a miracle, or murder, or both'. (CP140).

you rejoin Tess' walking route, having skirted to the north of the downland tracks described by Hardy.

From here on, it is road all the way to Beaminster: follow the description in Chapter XLIV of *Tess of the d'Urbervilles* for a roller-coaster ride over the hump-backed downs with fine views northwards across Blackmore Vale. En route you pass **Cross-in-Hand**, the stone monolith where Alec makes Tess swear a solemn oath (CP140), then the turning to Batcombe, home (now tomb) of 'Conjuror Mynterne'. Crossing Long-Ash Lane Tess reached Evershead, passing the Tanyard (barn where Alec preached), then the **Sow-and-Acorn inn** (avoided by Tess but visited in 'The First Countess of Wessex' and 'Interlopers'); beyond the church is Tess Cottage where she 'breakfasted a second time'. From Horsey Knap to Benville Bridge, Tess climbed to Toller Down Gate, crossing **Crimmercrock Lane** (CP201); *Far from the Madding Crowd* begins on the downland south of here: Hardy's **Norcombe**. Benvill Lane becomes the B3163 with consequent traffic hazards; at a bend on Storridge Hill is the gate where Tess paused to survey 'the basin in which **Emminster** (Beaminster) and its Vicarage lay' and the hedge where she stowed her thick walking boots. From the sleepy Market Square, Church Lane leads down to the mellow sandstone St Mary's with its graveyard of wild flowers. Beyond the Church in Barnes Lane the vicarage, now refurbished as 'The Beauty Room', has lost its uninviting chill.

Tess' last journey

After murdering Alec, Tess flees with Angel into the New Forest, where they hide for a while at **Bramhurst Manor** (Moyles Court), before fleeing northward along a route now designated the Avon Valley Way, passing by night through **Melchester** (Salisbury). To avoid detection Tess and Angel crept over old St Nicholas Bridge through that 'night as dark as a cave' on their fateful journey to 'solemn and lonely' Stonehenge, arrest and

Salisbury Cathedral, where Julian plays the organ in *The Hand of Ethelberta*.

imprisonment at Winchester (**Wintonchester**), where 'The President of the Immortals ended his sport with Tess'. 'From the western gate' the highway still climbs the Roman road, past Winchester Prison to the hilltop where Angel and Liza-Lu watched the black flag open upon the breeze.

Salisbury Cathedral is the setting of that important early poem 'The Impercipient' (CPs 44, 171, 667, 794); here also Julian plays the organ for Ethelberta. Across the tranquil close the Teacher Training College remains as a museum, its garden stretching down to the Avon, through which Sue Bridehead waded in flight from the oppressive regime; later to marry Phillotson in the nearby Church of St-Thomas-Becket. The cream-painted Georgian house at the north-eastern corner of the adjoining market square was the home of Edith Harman ('On the Western Circuit').

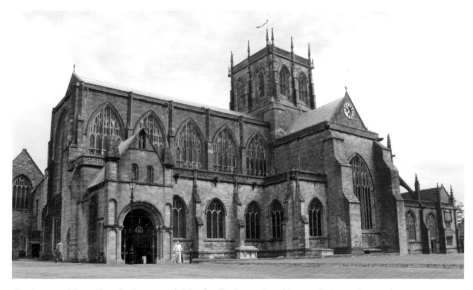

Sherborne Abbey Church: Grace and Giles 'walk about the abbey aisles' pondering the sorry circumstances 'to which a cruel fate has consigned them'. At the nearby market Winterbourne stood with 'his specimen apple-tree', rising above 'the heads of the farmers'.

Sherborne (**Sherton Abbas**) retains the air of an old-world market-town, where it is easy to imagine the grand front of Percomb's shop on Sheep Street with his tuppenny barber's premises in the yard behind. The market where Winterbourne displayed 'his specimen apple-tree' stood at the junction of Long and Cheap Streets, just east of the magnificent Abbey Church. (CP140). 'The chief hotel in Sherton Abbas, the Earl of Wessex', where honeymooning Grace spies Giles making cider in the yard outside, is now a Sherborne School boarding-house, first building on the left heading up from the station. Grace also visited Sherborne Castle, home of Lady Baxby, Hardy's Seventh Noble Dame.

Shaftesbury (**Shaston***)* seemed to young Tess a distant fairytale city as did *Christminster* to young Jude. Part 4 of *Jude,* begins with a detailed description of 'the ancient British Palladour', which will 'throw the visitor, into a pensive melancholy'. Jude enters the town 'after a toilsome climb' up cobbled Gold Hill (originally Cold Hill), turning left into Park Walk, from where there are fine views south over Blackmore Vale and then right into Bimport; on the northern side of which find 'Ox House' (**Old-Grove Place***)*, its ground floor sunk below street level, somewhat mitigating Sue's injuries in her leap from the bedroom window. Note nearby Jude Court.

NINE

North Wessex

In the summer of 1893 Hardy fell in love with Florence Henniker, resulting in a literary friendship which was to last her lifetime, rather than the passionate affair for which his heart was yearning. Between their meetings, he occupied his mind with the restoration of West Knighton Church and research in Oxfordshire and Berkshire (home of his paternal grandmother, Mary Head) for his final novel, *Jude the Obscure*: a restless peripatetic story in which the railway becomes a metaphor for the dysfunctional mobility of the modern age; the action driven by the railway timetable.

Part One: At Marygreen

Fawley, from which Jude derives his surname, is a sleepy agricultural community nestling in the north Berkshire Downs, where little appears to have changed from the major upheavals which Hardy decried following his visit in 1893:

'It was as old-fashioned as it was small . . . however, the well-shaft was probably the only relic of the local history that remained absolutely unchanged. Many of the thatched and dormered dwelling-houses had been pulled down of late years. The original church, hump-backed, wood-turreted, and quaintly hipped, had been taken down, and either cracked up into

Florence Henniker, who Hardy first met in Dublin in 1893 and with whom he became infatuated.

Jude's 'Vale of Brown Melancholy': 'in that ancient cornfield many a man had made love-promises to a woman at whose voice he had trembled by the next seed-time after fulfilling them in the church adjoining.'

heaps of road-metal in the lane, or utilized as pigsty walls, garden seats, and rockeries in the flower-beds of the neighbourhood. In place of it a tall new building of modern Gothic design, unfamiliar to English eyes, had been erected on a new piece of ground by a certain obliterator of historic records who had run down from London and back in a day'.

The church and its enclosing graveyard have mellowed with time, but still appear alien and peripheral to the village. From here, the rectory-house can be found 'round the corner' as described in the opening sentence of *Jude* and beside it the tiny school.

Some stones beside a beech tree at the eastern end of the green mark the village well; the cottages behind are the site of Aunt Drusilla's thatched cottage; steps opposite lead up to the Old Churchyard. The tarmac lane just past the Village Club is the original 'northward path' (now bridleway) leading to Farmer Troutham's field: that 'wide and lonely depression' 'sown as a cornfield' where for Jude the 'puny and sorry' lives of the rooks so much

The obliterated graves commemorated by eighteen-penny cast-iron crosses warranted to last five years'. These stout Victorian build crosses remain very much in evidence after 125 years.

The Milestone near the Brown House, on the back of which the young Jude chiselled 'Thither J.F.'; and beside which the phthisic older Jude lay down to rest.

resembled his own. The track curves up to join the Wantage (**Alfredston**) road; just north of this junction stood the isolated cottage, where Jude and Arabella acted out their brief marital cohabitation; the site of the pig-killing in the snow. All now obliterated under the plough as, due west from here, is a depression marking the 'large round pond', where the ice cracked under Jude but would not give way: 'he was not a sufficiently dignified person for suicide'.

Carefully follow the road uphill to the bend just beyond summit: the Brown House, onto the roof of which Jude climbed for a view of distant Oxford (**Christminster**), stood on the apex of the slope to your right beside the milestone, just before the turning to Letcombe Regis. Here from the ground, where all that remains of the barn is some hardcore amongst a rabbit-warren, 'the whole northern semicircle between east and west, to a distance of forty or fifty miles' is still spread before you. Opposite stood the gibbet 'not unconnected' with Jude's family history. 'Arabella's Cottage' in nearby Letcombe Bassett, is an immaculate large thatched house amongst the watercress beds: not a pig's pistle in sight, though the property would undoubtedly have met with Arabella's approval!

Part Two: At Christminster

Approaching Oxford with all the hesitant tenderness of a lover, Jude 'paused at the top of a crooked and gentle declivity, and obtained his first near view of the city': from Boars Hill to the south-west. To explore Jude's **Christminster**, start from Carfax, climb up the eponymous tower for a closer panorama of the city. This is Hardy's **Fourways**, where 'men had stood and talked of Napoleon, the loss of America, the execution of King Charles, the burning of the Martyrs, the Crusades, the Norman Conquest, possibly of the arrival of Caesar. Here the two sexes had met for loving, hating, coupling, parting; had waited, had suffered, for each other; had triumphed over each other; cursed each other in jealousy, blessed each other in forgiveness.'

Street maps showing all the sites associated with *Jude the Obscure* can be obtained from the Visitor Information Centre in Broad Street. Head south down St Aldates; to reach the magnificent facade of Christ Church (**Cardinal**) College, the entrance through Tom Tower,

Mildew Lane: 'a spot which to Jude was irresistible, though to Sue it was not so fascinating: a narrow lane close to the back of a college, but having no communication with it'.

whose bell sounded the 101-stroke curfew, counted by Jude on arrival in **Christminster**. Jude initially attended services in Christ Church Cathedral in hope of catching a glimpse of his as-yet-unknown cousin, Sue. In later disillusioned days, Jude mocks 'Cardinal with its long front, and its windows with lifted eyebrows, representing the polite surprise of the university at the efforts of such as I.'

Beyond Christ Church, turn left, then right to reach the banks of the Isis, follow around Christ Church Meadow with (in winter) extensive views of **Christminster**'s dreaming spires. Head for Oriel Square, passing Corpus Christi (**Tudor College**). In **Old-time Street**, Jude at work on Oriel (**Crozier**) College encounters Sue who looks 'right into his face with liquid untranslatable eyes'. Bear left into the High (**Chief Street**) to 'the church with the Italian porch', then Brasenose (**Rubric**) College and the Mitre (**Crozier Hotel**). Turn back down **Chief Street**; beyond St-Mary-the-Virgin is All Souls (**Sarcophagus**).

From the 'uncurtained window' of the lodging 'where she was not welcome' Sue contemplated 'the outer walls of Sarcophagus College: silent, black, and windowless' which 'threw their four centuries of gloom, bigotry, and decay into the little room she occupied, shutting out the moonlight by night and the sun by day'. Pass Queen's College, where Hardy received an Honorary Fellowship in June 1923, follow meandering Queen's Lane into New College Lane, together comprising **Mildew Lane**. Immediately before the 'Bridge of Sighs' a narrow alleyway (Hell Passage) leads to the 14th century Turf Tavern, the 'obscure tavern' where Jude lodged on the night his children died.

Above left 'The cross in the pavement which marked the spot of the Martyrdoms', that 'gloomy and inauspicious place' where Jude arranges to first meet Sue (see plaque on Balliol wall).

Above right The 'obscure and low-ceiled tavern' where Jude, drowned his sorrows before reciting the Nicene Creed in Latin. Later the same inn is 'entirely renovated and refitted in modern style', replete with Arabella as barmaid.

Ahead lies the Sheldonian Theatre, climbed by Jude for a (disillusioned) view 'over the whole town and its edifices'. On his final return to **Christminster**, Jude addressed 'a crowd of expectant people in the open space between this building and the nearest college' (Hertford). In Broad Street, find the Martyrs' Cross outside Balliol (**Biblioll**) College, whose Master offered Jude the 'terribly sensible advice' of 'remaining in your own sphere and sticking to your trade'. In response, Jude scrawled in chalk on the college wall 'I have understanding as well as you; I am not inferior to you: Yea, who knoweth not such things as these? - Job XII, 3'.

Turn up St Giles, past St John's College, to the Lamb and Flag: 'one of the great palpitating centres in Christminster life'. From here it is a short walk to the 'suburb nicknamed **Beersheba**' where Jude found 'on inexpensive terms the modest type of accommodation he demanded'. This is Jericho, built originally developed to house the workers of the Oxford University Press; at the intersection of Canal Street with St Barnabas stands the '**Church of Ceremonies: St Silas**', still 'the premier Anglo-Catholic Church in Oxford', from where Sue betrays her attendance by smelling of incense. St Barnabas remains ornate and beautifully decorated with its huge gilt cross suspended over the chancel steps. In nearby Walton Street, note the pub named Jude the Obscure; follow Walton Street to the gatehouse of St Sepulchre's Cemetery, where Jude's children were buried, a leafy and tranquil oasis amidst the 'urban roar': a place to pause and reflect, catch up on Jude or 'The Complete Poems' (CP578).

St Barnabas. 'High overhead, Jude could discern a huge, solidly constructed Latin cross; as large as the original it was designed to commemorate, suspended in the air by invisible wires. Underneath, lay what appeared to be a heap of black clothes.'

Wessex Heights

The 1890s was a difficult decade for Hardy: in 1892 his father died; in 1893 he fell in love with Florence Henniker but his advances were rejected; 1894 marked his twentieth wedding anniversary to the barren, uncompanionable, 'inconsequential' Emma; 1895 saw his fifty-fifth birthday and the completion of *Jude the Obscure*; in 1896 *Jude* was reviled by critics, burnt by the Bishop of Wakefield and withdrawn by W.H.Smith. Hardy sank into a deep dark depression, expressed in 'The Dead Man Walking' (CP166) and the In Tenebris sequence (CPs136-8), culminating in that cathartic piece of writing, often regarded as his finest poem, 'Wessex Heights' (CP261), completed on 14 December 1896. He names four specific Wessex Heights:

Ingpen (Inkpen) Beacon (970 feet): stands at the highest point on the ridge of hills running parallel to but south of Jude's North Wessex Ridgeway, separated by the valley of the River Kennet; here Berkshire, Hampshire and Wiltshire converge in an extensive panorama.

Wylls-Neck (Wills Neck) stands westwardly in the Quantocks (Coleridge country),

The view out over the Blackmore Vale from below Bulbarrow.

1,261 feet-above-sea-level: Hardy's wildest Wessex Height with views north across the Bristol Channel to Wales, east over the Somerset Levels and west to Exmoor.

Bulbarrow (902 feet), just north of Milton Abbas, is the third highest point in Dorset, and the views to the north out over the Blackmore Vale towards the Iron Age hilllfort of Hambledon Hill are some of the best in the county.

Pilsdon Crest (Pilsdon Pen), west of Beaminster (909 feet) near the Somerset and Devon borders, offers an unspoilt prospect southward across the Marshwood Vale to the sea (see the double page illustration at the start of this book, pages 2 and 3).

In 'Wessex Heights', the archetypal Hardyan protagonist stands alone on a series of hilltops, a spectator rather than an active participant in the world around him, the landscape beneath his feet populated by phantoms 'saying what I would not hear'; the poet unobserved but observing, where 'ghosts then keep their distance; and I know some liberty'.

TEN

Hardy's Wessex Place Names

Hardy's Name	Geographical Equivalent
Abbot's Cernel	Cerne Abbas
Abbotsea	Abbotsbury
Albrickham	Reading
Alderworth	Affpuddle Heath
Alfredston	Wantage
Anglebury	Wareham
Aquae Sulis	Bath
Athelhall	Athelhampton Hall
Barwith Strand	Trebarwith Strand
Beersheba	Jericho, Oxford
Blackbarrow	Rainbarrows
Blackon	Blackdown
Blooms-End	The Hardys' Cottage
Bramshurst Manor	Moyles Court
Budmouth	Weymouth
Budmouth Regis	Melcombe Regis
Bull-Stake Square	North Square
Camelton	Camelford
Carriford	West Stafford/ Lower Bockhampton
Carriford Road Station	Moreton
Casterbridge	Dorchester
Castle Boterel	Boscastle
Catknoll	Chetnole
Chalk Newton	Maiden Newton
Chalk Walk	Colliton Walk
Charmley	Charminster
Chaseborough	Cranborne
Christminster	Oxford
Cirque of the Gladiators	Maumbury Rings

Cliff Martin	Coombe Martin
Corvsgate	Corfe
Cresscombe	Letcombe Bassett
Creston	Preston
Crimmercrock Lane	A356 NW of Maiden Newton
Damer's Wood	Came Wood
Deadman's Bay	West Bay, Portland & Lyme Bay
Delborough	East Chelborough
Downstaple	Barnstaple
Dundagel	Tintagel
Durnover	Fordington
East Egdon	Affpuddle
East Endelstow	Lesnewth
East Mellstock	Lower Bockhampton
East Quarriers	Easton
Egdon Heath	Heath between Dorchester & Poole
Elensford	Islington, Puddletown
Emminster	Beaminster
Endelstow House	Lanhydrock
Enkworth Court	Encombe House
Evershead	Evershot
Exonbury	Exeter
Flintcomb-Ash	Plush
Flychett	Lychett Minster
Forest of the White Hart	Blackmore Vale
Froom-Everard	Stafford House
Glaston	Glastonbury
Great Forest	New Forest
Great Grey Plain	Salisbury Plain
Great Hintock	Melbury Osmund
Haggardon Hill	Eggardon Hill
Havenpool	Poole
Henry VIII's Castle	Sandsfoot Castle
Higher Crowstairs	Fiddlers Green
Hintock House	Melbury House
Holmstoke	East Stoke
Hope Cove	Church Ope Cove

Idmouth	Sidmouth
Ingpen	Inkpen
Isle of Slingers	Portland
Ivel(l)	Yeovil
Ivelchester	Ilchester
Kennetbridge	Newbury
Kingsbere(-sub-Greenhill)	Bere Regis
Kingscreech	Steeple
King's Hintock	Melbury Osmund
King's Hintock Court	Melbury House
Knapwater House	Kingston Maurward
Knollsea	Swanage
Leddenton	Gillingham
Lew-Everard	West Stafford
Lewgate	Higher Bockhampton
Little Enckworth	Kingston, Purbeck
Little Hintock	Melbury Bubb
Little Weatherbury Farm	Druce Farm
Little Welland	Winterbourne Zelston/ Milborne St Andrew
Longpuddle	Piddletrenthide & Piddlehinton
Longpuddle Church	All Saints, Piddletrenthide
Lower Longpuddle	Piddlehinton
Lower Mellstock	Lower Bockhampton
Lulwind/ Lulstead Cove	Lulworth Cove
Lumsdon	Cumnor
Maidon/ Mai Dun	Maiden Castle
Markton	Corfe and/ or Dunster
Marlott	Marnhull
Marshwood	Middlemarsh
Marygreen	Fawley, Berks
Melchester	Salisbury
Mellstock	Stinsford
Mellstock Cross	Bockhampton Cross
Middleton Abbey	Milton Abbas
Millpond St Jude	Milborne St Andrew
Mistover Knap	Green Hill
Mixen Lane	Mill Street, Fordington
Mount Lodge	Killerton House

Narrobourne	Hollywell, West Coker
Nether Moynton	Owermoigne
Newland Buckton	Buckton Newton
Norcombe Hill	Toller Down
Nuttlebury/ Nuzzlebury	Hazelbury Bryan
Oakbury Fitzpiers	Okeford Fitzpaine
Old-Grove Place	Ox House
Old Melchester	Old Sarum
Oozewood	Ringwood
Overcombe	Sutton Poyntz
Owlscombe	Batcombe
Oxwell Hall	Poxwell Hall
Peak Hill Cottage	Manor Gardens Cottage
Pebble Bank	Chesil Beach
Pen-Zephyr	Penzance
Peter's Finger	King's Head, Mill Street
Pilsdon Crest	Pilsdon Pen
Port Bredy	Bridport/ West Bay
Po'sham	Portesham
Pummery	Poundbury Hill Fort
Pure Drop Inn	The Crown, Marnhull
Pydel Vale	Piddle Valley
Quartershot	Aldershot
Quiet Woman Inn	Wild Duck/ Traveller's Rest
Red King's Castle	Rufus Castle
Ringsworth Shore	Ringstead Bay
Rou'tor Town	Bodmin
Roy-town	Troy Town
Rubdon Hill	Bubb Down
St Launce's	Launceston
St Silas	St Barnabas
Sandbourne	Bournemouth
Shaston	Shaftesbury
Shadwater Weir	Nine Hatches Weir, Ilsington
Sherton Abbas	Sherbourne
Shottsford Forum	Blandford Forum
Sleeping Green	Slepe and/ or Carhampton
Solentsea	Southsea,
Springham	Warmwell

Stancy Castle	Corfe Castle and/ or Dunster Castle
Stickleford	Tincleton
Stoke-Barehills	Basingstoke
Stourcastle	Sturminster Newton
Street of the Wells	Fortuneswell & Chiswell
Sylvania Castle	Pennsylvania Castle
Talbothays	Norris Mill Farm
Targan Bay	Pentargon Bay
The Beal	Portland Bill
The Chase	Cranborne Chase
The Island	Isle of Wight
The Ring	Maumbury Rings
The Slopes	Boveridge House
Tolchurch	Tolpuddle
Toneborough	Taunton
Tor-upon-Sea	Torquay
Trantridge	Boveridge
Tutcombe Bottom	Slutcombe Bottom
Upper Longpuddle	Piddletrenthide
Upper Mellstock	Higher Bockhampton
Valley of the Great Dairies	Frome Valley
Valley of the Little Dairies	Blackmore Vale
Vindilia	Portland
Warborne	Wimborne
Weatherbury	Puddletown
Weatherbury Farm	Waterston Manor
Welland Bottom	Ashley Bottom
Welland House	Charborough House and/ or Manor House, Milbourne
Welland Tower	Charborough Tower and/ or Rings Hill Speer
Wellbridge	Wool
Wellbridge Abbey	Bindon Abbey
West Endelstow	St Juliot
West Mellstock	Stinsford
West Shaldon	West Chaldon
Western Moor	Exmoor
Weydon Priors	Weyhill
Wintonchester	Winchester
Wylls-Neck	Wills Neck
Yalbury	Yellowham.

ELEVEN

The Characters in Hardy's Fiction

Name	Work
Abel Whittle	*The Mayor of Casterbridge*
Alec Stoke-d'Urberville	*Tess of the d'Urbervilles*
Angel Clare	*Tess of the d'Urbervilles*
Anne Garland	*The Trumpet-Major*
Ann-Avice (Avice II)	*The Well-Beloved*
Arabella Donn	*Jude the Obscure*
Aunt Drusilla	*Jude the Obscure*
Avice Caro	*The Well-Beloved*
Bathsheba Everdene	*Far from the Madding Crowd*
Betty Dornell	'The First Countess of Wessex'
Bob Loveday	*The Trumpet-Major*
Boldwood, Farmer	*Far from the Madding Crowd*
Burthen	'A Few Crusted Characters'
Clym Yeobright	*The Return of the Native*
Christine Everard	'The Waiting Supper'
Christoph Bless	'The Melancholy Hussar of the
German Legion'	
Conjuror Mynterne	*Tess of the d'Urbervilles*
Cytherea Aldclyffe	*Desperate Remedies*
Cytherea Graye	*Desperate Remedies*
Dick Dewy	*Under the Greenwood Tree*
Diggory Venn	*The Return of the Native*
Downe	'Fellow-Townsmen'
Dr Edred Fitzpiers	*The Woodlanders.*
Dr Grove	The Melancholy Hussar of the
German Legion'	
Edith Harman	'On the Western Circuit'
Elfride Swancourt	*A Pair of Blue Eyes*

Elizabeth-Jane Henchard — *The Mayor of Casterbridge*
Ethelberta Petherwin — *The Hand of Ethelberta*
Eustacia Vye — *The Return of the Native*

Fancy Day — *Under the Greenwood Tree*
Fanny Robin — *Far from the Madding Crowd*
Farfrae, Donald — *The Mayor of Casterbridge*
Farmer Lodge — 'The Withered Arm'
Farmer Troutham — *Jude the Obscure*
Felice Charmond — *The Woodlanders*

Gabriel Oak — *Far from the Madding Crowd*
George Melbury — *The Woodlanders*
Giles Winterbourne — *The Woodlanders*
Grace Melbury — *The Woodlanders*

Henchard, Michael — *The Mayor of Casterbridge*
Henery Fray — *Far from the Madding Crowd*

Joan Durbeyfield — *Tess of the d'Urbervilles*
John Loveday — *The Trumpet-Major*
Jopp — *The Mayor of Casterbridge*
Joseph Poorgrass — *Far from the Madding Crowd*
Jude Fawley — *Jude the Obscure*
Julian, Christopher — *The Hand of Ethelberta*

Knight, Henry — *A Pair of Blue Eyes*

Lady Baxby — 'Anna, Lady Baxby' (*A Group of Noble Dames*)
Liza-Lu Durbeyfield — *Tess of the d'Urbervilles*
Lucetta Le Sueur — *The Mayor of Casterbridge*
Lucy Savile — 'Fellow-Townsmen'

Marty South — *The Woodlanders*
Matilda Johnson — *The Trumpet-Major*
Mattheus Tina — 'The Melancholy Hussar of the German Legion'
Miss Aldclyffe — *Desperate Remedies*
Mop Ollamoor — 'The Fiddler of the Reels'
Mother Cuxsom — *The Mayor of Casterbridge*
Mr Grinham — *Under the Greenwood Tree*
Mr Maumbury — 'A Changed Man'

Mrs Yeobright	*The Return of the Native*
Nicholas Long	*'The Waiting Supper'*
Owen Graye	*Desperate Remedies*
Parson Maybold	*Under the Greenwood Tree*
Percomb	*The Woodlanders*
Phillotson, Richard	*Jude the Obscure*
Pierston, Jocelyn	*The Well-Beloved*
Power, Paula	*A Laodicean*
Revd Clare	*Tess of the d'Urbervilles*
Sergeant Troy	*Far from the Madding Crowd*
Shepherd Fennel	*'The Three Strangers'*
Stephen Reynard	*'The First Countess of Wessex'*
Stephen Smith	*A Pair of Blue Eyes*
Sorrow Durbeyfield	*Tess of the d'Urbervilles*
Sue Bridehead	*Jude the Obscure*
Susan Henchard / 'Newson'	*The Mayor of Casterbridge*
Tess Durbeyfield	*Tess of the d'Urbervilles*
Thomasin Yeobright	*The Return of the Native*
Tranter Reuben	*Under the Greenwood Tree*
Widow Jethway	*A Pair of Blue Eyes*
Wildeve, Damon	*The Return of the Native*

Acknowledgements and Further Reading

My thanks for the help given by George Wickham at the Dorset County Museum; to my colleagues at The Thomas Hardy Society; to my partner Mary for her continued patient support; to Eddie and Lizzie for their enthusiastic investigation of the walks; to Russell Butcher for instigating this project, and David Burnett at the Dovecote Press for his endless patience, advice and hard work in bringing it to fruition.

I would also like to thank the following for allowing the inclusion of illustrations in their possession or for which they hold the copyright: Dorset County Museum: pages 9, 15 (Hardy painting), 25, 30 (lower), 33, 42 (Henry Moule painting), 46 (left), rear cover. Fitzwilliam Museum, Cambridge: 55 (lower).Dovecote Press: pages 7, 11 (lower), 22, 37, 38, 44, 46 (right), 50, 53 (lower), 58, 62, 66, 68, 73, 79. Guy Fincham: front cover, pages 27 (map), 28 (right). Peter Lightfoot: all maps except that on page 27. Peter Rushworth: page 30 (upper). Simon Ellis: page 43. All the other illustrations are my own.

Suggested Further Reading

Bullen, J.B., *Thomas Hardy, the World of His Novels* (Frances Lincoln, 2013)
Fincham, Tony, *Hardy's Landscape Revisited* (Robert Hale, 2010)
Ed. Gibson, James, *The Complete Poems of Thomas Hardy* (Macmillan, 1976)
Kay-Robinson, Denys, *Hardy's Wessex Re-appraised* (David & Charles, 1972)
Millgate, Michael, *Thomas Hardy A Biography* (OUP,1982)

The Thomas Hardy Society

www.hardysociety.org   Email: info@hardysociety.org